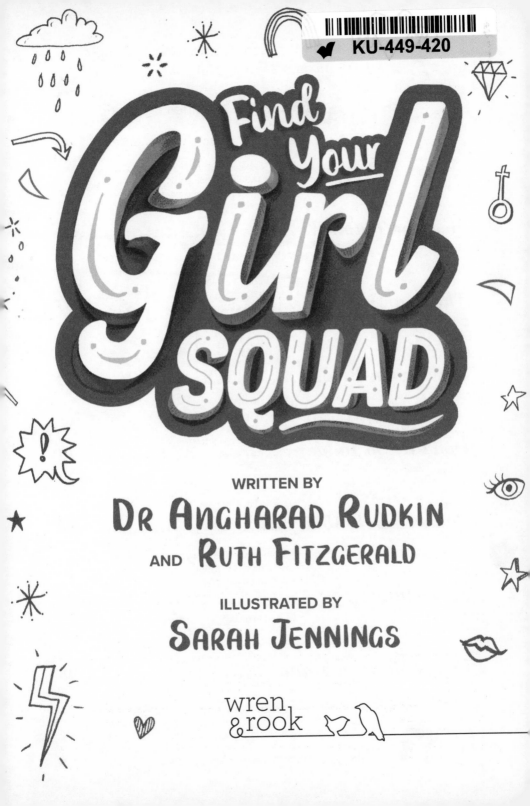

Find Your Girl SQUAD

WRITTEN BY

Dr Angharad Rudkin
AND **Ruth Fitzgerald**

ILLUSTRATED BY

Sarah Jennings

wren & rook

Contents

To my very own girl squad. You know who you are
and you are wonderful – A.R.

For Edie – the first and best guinea pig – R.F.

First published in Great Britain in 2020 by Wren & Rook

ISBN: 978 1 5263 6250 6
E-book ISBN: 978 1 5263 6251 3
10 9 8 7 6 5 4 3 2 1

MIX
Paper from
responsible sources
FSC® C104740

Wren & Rook
An imprint of
Hachette Children's Group
Part of Hodder & Stoughton
Carmelite House
50 Victoria Embankment
London EC4Y 0DZ

An Hachette UK Company
www.hachette.co.uk
www.hachettechildrens.co.uk

Publishing Director: Debbie Foy
Managing Editor: Liza Miller
Art Director: Laura Hambleton
Designed by Fabiana Guglielmi

Printed in the UK

Additional images supplied by Shutterstock

Contents

Meet the Team

FRIENDS.

What does that word make you think of? The great group of mates that you hang out with every day? Fun, laughter and sharing? A cheesy 90s sitcom that you have to admit is still hilarious?

Or maybe, if you're like most people, it means a roller-coaster ride of good times and not so good times; fun stuff and mean stuff; being in the group and then out of it again.

Notice the words 'most people' there – because, no matter what people tell you or how they act, everyone struggles with friendships at some time or other.

So, if the word 'friends' is making you think

at the moment – don't panic! We are here to help!

And together, we are the Squad Finders! A.K.A. ...

Angharad: SquF? Really?
Ruth: I know. It needs work.

The good news is that human beings are designed to be sociable. Back in the old cavegirl days, we could never have survived without our tribe to help and protect us.

Imagine. There you are outside your cave in a buffalo skin onesie, waving your club and shouting, 'Ain't no woolly mammoth gonna stomp on my campfire!' and all your fierce cavegirly friends are there to back you up, saying 'Too right, sister!' as the woolly mammoth slopes off to find an easier dinner. (Note: do not quote this in a history test.)

And though we may not all walk round waving clubs and grunting any more (not unless we're in a really bad mood), things are not so different now. We need friends to support us, to stick up for us, to cheer us up and cheer us on, and to lend us fifty pence for a chocolate bar.

Humans can only survive and thrive by living in a group.

BUT.

Working out how to find your place in that group, who your friends are and how to find your true Girl Squad can be a

COMPLETE NIGHTMARE!

Here at **SQUF!** Headquarters (or Angharad's kitchen table as it's sometimes called), we are on a mission to help you find your way through the friendship maze. We know that if you want to fit in with friends, it can sometimes feel like you have to change and act like someone else, so we have been finding out the best ways to create great friendship groups, having fun and still being who you want to be.

Sounds like a tall order, right?

NO!

Because guess what? It turns out that there are (cue deep, rumbly voice)

Super Psychology Secrets!

to help us learn how to make and keep good friends. Once you understand how these

Super Psychology Secrets!

work, then you will be on your way to

AMAZETASTIC FRIENDSHIP-NESS-DOM!

This is a highly scientific term, we don't expect you to memorise it.

Now, before we go any further, there's something we need to say.

People are weird.

Also: **KIND** **FUNNY** *Friendly*

SHY

GRUMPY **SILLY** **SULKY** **GIGGLY**

and a lot of other stuff that sounds like a
list of Snow White's housemates. Everyone
in the world is a mixture of all these things
and loads more. And everyone is completely unique.
A one-off.

AN INDIVIDUAL.

Ahh! **You say.** *But what about the Barker twins in my school?
They are identical. Even their mother can't tell them apart.
Sometimes even they get confused which twin they are.* **But
even identical twins, who may look the same on the outside,
have different things going on on the inside.**

You see, your brain is a bit like your body. Obviously, it
doesn't look the same, it's kind of grey and cauliflower-
shaped (unless you actually are a cauliflower, in which
case – wow! We have vegetable readers!) but, just like your
body, some of the way your brain works comes from the
genes you were born with, while a whole lot more is the
result of the environment it's been living in and the things
it's taken in.

Your brain absorbs influences from all around you. From your parents and family of course, but also from friends, films, books, music, celebrities, sports, pets, songs, TV adverts, magazines, video games and stuff written on cereal packets – the list of things battling to influence how we think is endless. But not just that. Our brains also learn from experience.

Imagine a little girl, four years old. One day, after weeks of trying, she manages to climb to the top of the little kids' climbing frame in the park. She feels great! After a few weeks, she gets the confidence to tackle the big kids' climbing frame and, a few years later, the climbing wall at the sports centre. One day, who knows – she might climb Everest!

BUT.

Now imagine the same little girl. What if, instead of getting to the top of the little kids' climbing frame, she falls off and bangs her knee? She might decide to give up on climbing frames altogether. Never mind the climbing wall. Forget Everest. She'll probably take up knitting instead.

Everything that happens to us shapes us. And that's before we even get to hormones and peer pressure and social media and what your Gran's next-door neighbour says. And that is why we're all different.

All this is good stuff, really. Imagine how dull the world would be if everyone was exactly the same. Imagine if everyone wore beige, talked like the prime minister and ate only peas and potatoes. (Apologies if this sounds like you. That's fine. Go you! And thank goodness you're unique.) We're meant to be different – and the world's a much more interesting place because of this.

BUT.

That also means that it can be difficult to understand how people act sometimes – after all, we haven't had their influences, so trying to figure out what's going on in their heads is never going to be easy.

In fact, never mind other people, it can sometimes be difficult to know why *we* act like we do. For example, why is it that one day, you can have the best laugh having a singalong in the car with your family and the next day even hearing them speak makes you annoyed and all you want to do is sit in your room with a sign on the door saying

Where were we? Right, we can't change how other people are, and we shouldn't try. Trying to change or control someone's behaviour does not set you on the track to

It just makes you a bit annoying, at best. But there are ways we can teach ourselves to think, and behaviours we can learn, that influence how people react to us. And that brings us back to our

Angharad: Can I stop doing that voice now? It's making my throat hurt.

OK. Let's get on with it.

Chapter One

No, wait a minute – before we move on, there is something else we need. As with any scientific study, we will need a guinea pig.

Not that sort of guinea pig. Someone to help us explain the concepts as they come up. An ordinary girl, with ordinary friends in an ordinary school.

We advertised for the post and one application came flooding in.

SQUF!

GUINEA PIG APPLICATION FORM

Please fill in your details below:

Name: Poppy

Hair: yes

Eyes: Two

Height: Sort of middley, short-ish

School: Pilkington Rd

Family: One mum. One very annoying younger brother

Friends:

YUUUUURGH!!

Clearly a person in need of our help!

Poppy, you've got the job. Now, onwards.

The Brand of You

In her role as guinea pig, Poppy has agreed to record a video diary every day about her friendship problems, and send it in to SQUF! HQ for us to discuss.

In fact, I think there's one coming through right now ... Let's go live to the PoppyCam!

POPPYCAM

REC

Hello Team SQUF! It's me, Poppy, on the PoppyCam. Can you hear me?

Loud and clear, Poppy. How was your day?

Oh dear.

So, it wasn't a brilliant start to Monday morning. My little brother stole the last of the Chokko-Pops – I mean, he actually set his alarm so he could get up before me to get to them. Then Mum told me off for telling him off. Then she told me off again for being 'deliberately slow' putting my shoes on – as if that's a thing. I was probably just totally energy-less from having to eat sawdust for breakfast, or muesli as Mum calls it.

I'm walking into school when I spot Jada ahead of me, and for once Izzy isn't already with her. I run to catch up with her but only manage to say, 'Did you have a good weeke–' when this blood-curdling scream comes from behind us and Izzy is galloping up the road, wailing 'Giiiiiiiirls! Did you see it? Did you see it?'

'Err. What?!' I say, looking around in case I've missed a low-flying spaceship or something.

'Glam Girls of course!'

I must look a bit blankish because she says, 'The new reality TV show? About the girls training to be make-up artists?'

'Err … I don't think so,' I say.

'It was only last night, Poppy,' Izzy snaps, 'Even you can't be that dozy.'

I didn't watch it of course. A show about trainee make-up artists sounds about as

exciting as cold spaghetti.
Anyway, my mum wanted
to watch The Secrets of
the Universe, which was
actually really interesting. Did
you know that there are more stars in the
universe than there are grains of sand on all the beaches
on Earth?! My brain hurts just thinking about it.

For a very crazy nano-second I consider telling Izzy and
Jada this, but then I realise that unless perfect cheekbone
contouring is one of the secrets of the universe, they
wouldn't be interested.

'I saw Glam Girls,' Jada says, 'It was really cool.' And they do this smile at each other as if they have a special secret that I don't understand.

That happens all the time, lately.

The thing is, Jada and me have been friends since we were in Reception. On our first day at school, she brought her Elsa doll and I brought my Olaf the snowman toy and that was it. We were best friends. We kind of grew out of playing with dolls (although Olaf still lives at the end of my bed), but we still sometimes have sleepovers where we watch Disney films and eat popcorn and sing – just for fun. Or we did. Until Izzy came to our school and somehow everything changed.

'Wait, wait,' Izzy says. 'I've just had one of my brilliant ideas! Why don't we rename our Girl Squad ...

THE GLAM SQUAD?!'

'Eww! That sounds—'

I am about to say awful, when I realise that Jada is already hopping up and down squealing, 'We are the Glam Squad! We are the Glam Squad!'

'Yeah. That sounds great,' I say.

It's not that I don't like Izzy. She can be fun and she's really brave too. She's the sort of person who never worries about asking a dinner lady for extra chips, and last week she put her hand up in class when Mrs Lambert *was going on about Henry VIII again and said, 'Miss, this is so boring. Why can't we do some interesting royals like Harry and Meghan instead?'*

Everybody laughed, even Mrs Lambert. I'll bet if I'd have said that I'd have got a minus point. That's the trouble, everyone seems to think Izzy's cool. She calls herself the leader of the Girl Squad, I mean Glam Squad (yuck!), and everyone wants to hang out with her. Especially Jada.

The Squad is Izzy, Jada, Bea, Anna, me and a couple of others and if you're not in the Squad, you miss out on stuff like parties and chat groups, and also, if you're not in her Squad, Izzy can be kind of mean.

Anyway, while I'm standing there trying not to mention supernovas, Izzy suddenly holds her hand up and says, 'Wait! I've just had another one of my brilliant ideas!'

And Jada gets all, 'Oooh, tell me! Tell me!'

Izzy says, 'You know my sleepover on Friday?'

Of course we know, she's been going on about it for weeks, and she keeps changing who's invited. Amelia Munnings has been on and off the list three times already.

'Let's make it a Glam Girls sleepover!' Izzy says.

'OMG! That's so brilliant,' Jada says, doing little jumps around the place.

'Yes. We can give you a makeover, Poppy!' Izzy says, giving me a not-very-smiley smile.

I try to say no but I only get as far as 'Oh, I don't really like–' when Jada loudly interrupts.

'Don't be so lame, Poppy! It will be fun.'

'Unless you don't want to come?' Izzy says, opening her eyes wide. 'I'll cross you off my list if you like.'

So I say quickly, 'No, no. Only joking. Can't wait.'

But the thing is, I don't want to watch Glam Girls, or get a makeover. In fact, I don't even want to go to the sleepover much. It will just be Izzy showing off. But if I don't go then Izzy will be mad at me and say I can't be in her Squad any more. And then I'll lose Jada completely and have no friends at all.

So that's why I feel

Can you help me, Team **SQUF!**?

Oh dear! Poor Poppy. This looks like the perfect case for the first of our ...

WHAT'S YOUR BRAND?

Poppy's suffering from what we at **SQUF!** call 'going off-brand'. We all have times when we say we like, or don't like, things just to fit in. And not just TV programmes. It happens with bands, clothes, hairstyles – all sorts of things. People like to belong to a group. Up to a point, this is natural. It can help you bond with your friends and find new interests.

The trouble comes when we try so hard to fit in that we forget to be our **real self**. That's when we can start to feel very uncomfortable. It might not matter too much when it comes to which TV show we watch, but what about when we have to decide how we act, or how we treat other people, or even how we treat ourselves? These decisions are too important just to go along with the crowd.

So now we have another problem. How do we understand what our **real self** is?

As we have already talked about, humans are made up of many different bits. In the same way that we all have different physical characteristics – red hair, brown eyes, really weird earlobes – we all enjoy different things and have

different interests and talents. And this is important to keep the world working. The world needs people who love make-up to become make-up artists, people who love cooking to become chefs, and people who are fascinated by space to become astronomers. So, having differences is not only natural, it's essential.

A good way of thinking about what makes your **real self** is to think about your values.

Values describe what's really important to you. They are the things that make you, you. Kind of like your brand.

Values are usually described in one or two words such as **KIND, FUN, CREATIVE, HARD-WORKING.** Words that explain what matters to you, what gives meaning to your life and what gives it a sense of purpose.

Here's a list of some values.

Take a look through and think about which ones are important to you. Then choose your top three or so. Don't think about it too hard as it's very easy to tie yourself up in knots deciding, just pick a few that you think sum up what matters most to you. If one of your values isn't listed here then just give it a simple name, add it to your list and make it one of yours.

ACCEPTANCE

COURAGE

SAFETY

Neatness

Cooperation

Beauty

SELF-CONTROL

HONESTY

FAIRNESS

CHALLENGE

Generosity

FRIENDLINESS

Kindness

CURIOSITY

ADVENTURE

Gratitude

TRUST

SKILFULNESS

CONTROL

RESPECT

PATIENCE

Humour

Freedom

CREATIVITY CARING

ENJOYMENT

DETERMINATION

Fitness

EXCITEMENT LOVE ♡

Now you have your top three values. What does that tell you? Knowing your values can help you decide what to focus on and what you'd rather let go. They help you decide where to put your energies and how to understand other people. They give you direction.

If your list of values contains **CURIOSITY, KNOWLEDGE** and **ADVENTURE**, you might be the kind of person who finds travel really exciting, while your friend might prefer nights at home in front of the TV, especially if her values include **Family**, **SAFETY** and **ENJOYMENT**.

Does it mean one of you is wrong or boring? No, it just means you have different interests and values, which we've already seen is a good thing. Does it mean you can't be friends? Of course it doesn't! Accept you will have differences as well as things in common and this will make you even better friends. Over time, it may mean that you also find other friends who have similar values to yours.

Jada used to like the same sort of things as Poppy and valued their friendship, but now she's changing. Values can change over time, especially when we're young. For example, toddlers and young children are usually very self-centred. They haven't yet learned to share and be sociable and may snatch toys away from other children. When they grow up, they begin to realise that it's more fun to play games with others, and share things.

Izzy seems to have **CONTROL** as one of her values. This just means she likes to be in charge. It can be a good thing in some circumstances. It wouldn't be a lot of use having a headteacher or a prime minister who didn't want to take decisions, but in different circumstances it can be difficult to cope with. Some people seem happy to be 'bossed around' by their friend – perhaps one of their values is being **AGREEABLE** – but most people don't like it and just put up with it because they're worried about being pushed out of the group.

Getting to know your values is like knowing your

True Brand.

And once you are confident of your brand, you can start to live a life that's truer to you.

According to research, people who live in harmony with their values are believed to be happier and more content and to feel that their lives are meaningful and make sense.

So, finding your values and staying on-brand sounds like a great idea. Perhaps you could give it a try, Poppy? Go for it!

POPPYCAM

REC

OK. So I've looked at the list and first of all I thought about twenty of the values were mine. But now I've thought about it a bit more I've narrowed it down to the really important stuff.

I really value FRIENDSHIP but now things have changed and I'm not quite sure who my friends are. I hate it when people tell lies and cheat at games and stuff,

so I think another of my real values is HONESTY. Only, it's hard to be honest. If I say I don't like Glam Girls, there'll just be another reason for them to laugh at me. And maybe CREATIVITY because I love drawing and art. Jada used to too, but now she says it's a bit childish, so I mostly do it at home.

So, I think the Brand of Poppy is FRIENDSHIP, HONESTY and CREATIVITY. But I don't see how this helps me – knowing that isn't making me feel any better right now.

Anyway, that's my video diary for tonight. I'm switching off the PoppyCam now. My mum's bought some more Chokko-Pops and I need to find somewhere to hide them.

Hmm. It seems pretty clear that Poppy's values don't really fit in with what's happening around her. She values friendship, but Jada doesn't seem that friendly any more. She values honesty, but is she really being honest by pretending to like things she doesn't enjoy? And what's happened to the fun she used to have being creative with her art?

She's totally

OFF-*brand*

and that's why she's feeling so uncomfortable. Poppy needs to make some decisions to get back on track, and she can use her values to help her make the right ones for her.

Staying On-Brand

Staying true to our personal brand involves making decisions. We make hundreds of decisions every day, from what socks to wear, to where to sit at lunchtime, to whether to tell the art teacher that her new glasses make her look like a frog. (Tip: don't.)

Most decisions are subconscious, meaning we only have to use a tiny bit of our brains to make them. You probably don't spend ten minutes trying to decide whether to eat your soup with a spoon or a fork. Some decisions need a lot more brain power though, such as whether to put your hand up to answer a question in class, whether to make an effort to speak to the new girl, or what to wear to a party.

One of the great things about knowing your values is that they can help to guide your decisions. And that can be very useful, especially if you find yourself in a difficult situation where you're not sure what to do for the best.

If **CHALLENGE** and **hard-working** are included in your values list, then answering that question in class might be the right thing for you to do, even if you feel uncomfortable doing it, because it's in line with your values. If **CARING** and **FRIENDSHIP** feature in your personal brand, then overcoming the awkwardness and chatting to the new girl will make you feel great about yourself.

Sometimes knowing our values can help us not to make bad decisions too. If one of our values is **fitness**, this might encourage us to steer clear of unhealthy sweets and snacks, or a value of **FAIRNESS** can remind us to think twice before copying in a test.

Oh! We've got an incoming video.

POPPYCAM

REC

How was your day today, Poppy?

UUUUUURGH?!

Oh dear.

Tuesday morning got off to a much better start –
I actually got a decent breakfast. (Hiding the Chokko-
Pops in the washing basket was an act of genius, even
if I do say so myself. My brother never puts anything in
it. I don't even think he knows we have one.) I thought
a lot more about my values last night. I'm happy that
friendship, honesty and creativity are three of mine. And
finding that out makes me feel good about myself because
they're the sorts of things I like in other people too.

I think the creativity bit came out in my history
homework, which I was secretly pretty pleased with.
We had to write about Henry VIII. I wrote:

Henry VIII was King of England in the 1500s. At that time
they thought the Sun revolved around the Earth. Then a
Polish scientist called Nicolaus Copernicus found out that the
Earth and other planets moved around the Sun. He is often
called the father of modern astronomy – Nicolaus, I mean.
Henry didn't know this stuff.

I thought she might give me an extra mark for
background research. I like to put something a bit
different in my homework, it makes teachers think.

But as it turned out, including Mr Copernicus was a very
bad mistake.

I get a message from Jada first thing, saying she's off sick
with a cold. I'm sure Izzy won't bother to hang out with
me without Jada around, so I'm kind of surprised when

Hi she catches up with me on the way into school and says, 'Hi Pops!'

'Hi,' I say. 'Jada's off sick.'

'Yes I know, she messaged me,' Izzy says. And, though I know it doesn't really matter, I can't help wishing that Jada had only messaged me.

'Never mind,' Izzy says. 'We can walk together. Look, I've got a new bag,' she says, holding it up. It's one of those really expensive handbags. 'My dad got it for me.' She grins.

Izzy's parents split up last year. They always seem to compete about who can buy her the best stuff. That's why she's getting to have a big sleepover at her mum's when it's not even her birthday.

'It's really nice,' I say.

'I'm so glad you're coming to my sleepover, you know?' She gives me a big smile.

I find myself smiling back without even meaning to. My face just sort of takes over and I get this happy, fuzzy feeling inside. That's the thing about Izzy, when she's nice to you, you feel sort of special, like you're really part of her Squad.

'I've had a bit of a nightmare though,' she says and then she really surprises me by linking her arm through mine and leaning in as if she's about to tell me a secret. I catch

Amelia Munnings looking over and can't help giving her a little smile. I know this is mean of me really, because she got crossed off the sleepover list again yesterday, but there's another bit of me that wants everyone to see me being friends with Izzy.

'No, really. It's honestly so annoying but I've gone and left my homework behind, again,' Izzy says.

'What, the Henry VIII stuff?' I ask, trying not to sound disappointed. I was hoping for a slightly more exciting secret.

'Yeah. I'm so worried. Mrs Lambert's going to be so mad.'

I'm a bit surprised at this. Mrs Lambert's not the so mad type. She's more of a Hmm-try-harder-next-time kind of teacher.

'She'll probably be OK if you explain and promise to bring it in tomorrow,' I say.

'No, you don't get it. It's the fourth time I've forgotten my homework this term. Last time she got the hump and said I'd get a detention next.'

'Maybe you could just quickly write it out again,' I say. 'It's only a couple of pages.'

'But I can't remember what I wrote! I mean, I can't help it – I've got this really bad memory. Probably I should see a doctor about it.'

'Have you?' I say. I haven't heard her mention this before. Although come to think of it, she did forget my birthday.

'Yeah. You could help me out though,' she says. 'Perhaps I could just have a look at what you've written?'

My nice fuzzy feeling quickly drains away. 'But you can't put the same as me ... I don't think we're allowed.'

Izzy unlinks her arm from mine and looks at me with a shocked expression. 'I'm not going to copy it!' she says. 'I just need a memory boost.'

'I don't know,' I say. But I do know. Izzy doesn't think there's anything wrong with copying someone else. She copied Noora's maths test last week – I saw her looking over Noora's shoulder – and once she got Priti Begum to do her science homework by promising to invite her to her birthday party. Then she didn't.

But Izzy is still going on. 'You would if you were a real friend,' she says, sounding all hurt. 'After all, I am inviting you to my sleepover.'

And then I start to worry. If I don't let her see it, she might cross me off the sleepover list, or even throw me out of the Glam Squad altogether.

With a quick check to make sure Amelia Munnings isn't looking, I slip my folder into her bag.

And she gives me her big smile again. 'You're a star, Pops! I won't be long,' she says, and she skips off.

When I get into class a little later, I find my folder on my table with my homework inside.

Perhaps she did just glance at it, I think, I'm probably worrying over nothing. I hand it in to Mrs Lambert.

At lunchtime Izzy saves the seat next to her at the Glam Squad table. 'Sit here, Poppy,' she says, and I can't help smiling when I see Bea and Anna looking huffy.

But after lunch is when it all goes wrong.

Mrs Lambert calls me and Izzy in from lunch break early. 'Can I just have a word, girls?' she says. And the way she says it makes me think it's not going to be a very enjoyable word.

'I was very impressed with your homework, Poppy,' she says, but she doesn't smile.

'I was also very impressed with your homework, Izzy.'

'Thank you, Mrs Lambert,' Izzy says.

'My problem is,' Mrs Lambert continues, as if Izzy hasn't spoken, 'that you seem to have exactly the same homework, right down to a certain Polish astronomer.'

I bite my lip. I can't believe Izzy mentioned Copernicus. She must have copied it word for word.

'Someone here has clearly been copying,'
Mrs Lambert says.

'No way,' Izzy says. 'I'm not a cheat!'

Mrs Lambert turns to me. 'Poppy?'

'I … I … ' I stutter, not knowing what to say.

'I'd like to know which one of you wrote this first and
who copied. If you don't own up, I'm afraid you will both
get a minus mark and another essay to complete tonight.'

I look at Izzy. She says nothing, just twists up her lips
and stares out the window.

'Very well. I must say I'm very disappointed in you both,' Mrs Lambert says. And I feel awful. Mrs Lambert is such a nice teacher and I worked really hard on that homework.

On the way out, Mrs Lambert calls me back.

'I'm pretty sure I know what happened here, Poppy,' she says, 'But you need to learn that if you let someone copy your work, you are just causing more problems for yourself.'

Of course, once we got outside Izzy didn't even apologise for getting us in trouble.

'She probably wouldn't have noticed if you hadn't put that stupid Coppernut stuff in!' she says.

'It's Copernicus,' I say, but it doesn't matter because she's already turned and walked away.

So that's my video diary for today. Everything is still

Only now it's

with added extra homework.

Hmm. Things don't really seem to be improving for Poppy, do they? She's worked out her values: **FRIENDSHIP**, **CREATIVITY** and **HONESTY**. The trouble is she didn't stick to them very well. Letting Izzy copy her homework didn't exactly fit with being honest and she wasn't very friendly to Amelia.

Now she feels that she's let down her teacher and herself. No wonder she's still feeling

The thing about values is that finding them is the easy bit, while actually living by them can be hard. When people are confident and popular, like Izzy, it can be difficult to stand up to them. And it doesn't have to be someone mean. It can be just as difficult to tell your really good friends that you don't want to go along with them.

For example, what if you are at a sleepover and someone suggests watching a horror film? Maybe *Alien Zombie Clown Invasion* is your favourite movie. But what if it's not? What if you're the sort of person who has sleepless nights after watching a particularly dramatic episode of *Blue Planet*?

Finding the confidence to communicate how you feel can seem impossible when everyone else feels differently, but there are ways that can help.

Learning to state what you want calmly and clearly is called being assertive, or as we like to call it here at **SQUF!**, being stand-uppy. Some people confuse being stand-uppy with being bossy or rude, but it's very different. You can still be stand-uppy while being perfectly polite. Think of it as protecting your brand.

There are a few things that can help you to say something in a stand-uppish way.

1 **TAKE THE 'PERSONAL' PART OUT.**
You are not saying you don't like your friend, just the activity.
'I love watching films with you guys, but...'

2 **STATE CLEARLY WHAT YOU DO OR DON'T LIKE OR WANT.** 'Horror films make me scared and give me nightmares.'

3 **IF POSSIBLE, MAKE AN ALTERNATIVE SUGGESTION.** 'How about we watch *The Greatest Showman* and have a singalong?'

Super SQUF! tip:
This helps give the others a way out of the situation so they don't get all defensive.

4 **USE REPETITION.** At first people might talk over you or not listen, so don't be afraid to repeat what you said, in a slightly louder voice. 'Like I said, I can't watch this film, so we need to find a different one.

3 **FIND THE HUMOUR.** If you're still feeling awkward, and it's not a serious situation, then sometimes humour can help. 'I love you girls, but if you make me watch that film I will probably wet myself and cry for my mummy. Let's watch *The Greatest Showman*.'

6 GET PREPPED. A good idea to help with being stand-uppy is to work out a few phrases to help you get started. Things like, 'I don't agree with that idea. I think...' or 'When you do XXX it makes me feel unhappy/anxious/as if you're not listening to me.'

The really important thing to remember is that you **don't need to apologise** for saying what you want or don't want to happen.

Many of us, particularly girls, tend to start sentences with, 'I'm sorry, but...' As if what you think is not as important as what other people think. But starting this way instantly makes it seem as if we *have* something to apologise for – and of course there's no need to say sorry for listening to your values and making choices based on what you feel and believe to be right.

So, practise your stand-uppiness, because you have a great brand, what you think matters, and the world needs to hear it!

Now, there's something we haven't fully explained about the PoppyCam. It has built-in Mega **SQUF!** technology, which lets us rewind and imagine how things might have gone in a different way. What if Poppy had worked out how to be more stand-uppy with Izzy? Let's rewind to the point where Izzy asks for Poppy's homework.

POPPYCAM

Rewind.

'*I'm not going to copy it!*' *Izzy says.*

'*I just need a memory boost.*'

'*I don't know,*' *I say.*

'*You would if you were a real friend,*' *she says, sounding all hurt. '*After all, I am inviting you to my sleepover.*'

We'll just stop there, before Poppy hands over her folder. Izzy is using lots of tricks to get Poppy to do what she wants. She makes her feel as if she is being a bad friend; she pretends Poppy is hurting her feelings; and she reminds Poppy that she has something Poppy wants (the sleepover).

Let's see what happens when Poppy is more stand-uppy:

POPPYCAM

REC

'*It's got nothing to do with our friendship, Izzy. I'm looking forward to your party. But I'm just the sort of person who feels very uncomfortable breaking school rules. Perhaps I could come with you to help explain to Mrs Lambert?*' *I say.*

'*Oh just forget it, Poppy!*' *Izzy says.*

Izzy is still cross, but she was going to be anyway, and it's difficult for her to be *too* angry when Poppy is offering to help her in another way. Poppy can feel good about herself and she avoids all the unpleasantness with Mrs Lambert.

Surprisingly, when we are true to ourselves, people tend to like us better, not less. It may take them a little time to adjust, but once other people know what to expect, they will respect you for being consistently **YOU**. And don't forget – they're trying to work out who they are too!

Being assertive takes practice, and it's not easy, but it can help you out in some tough situations when you need to stand up for your values – because in the long run, you'll always feel happier when you do.

Spend some time working out who you really are and what you really value, stand up for those values and *get on-brand*.

THE BRAND OF YOU.

Don't Be So Judgey

POPPYCAM

REC

Hello Team **SQUF!** .

Look. I've got a bit of a thing I want to say.

Ahem. Here goes.

I value your support, and I know you want to help, BUT I thought you were going to help me to be part of the Squad and instead I seem to be getting into more and more trouble with Izzy. I totally get that knowing my values is helpful, but perhaps we could look at something else now.

By the way, I think the assertiveness methods are working.

Gosh! Go Poppy! That was very assertive. Give yourself a house point/merit mark/gold star/cupcake with extra sprinkles (delete as appropriate).

Poppy's right, we do need to move on to the next

And for this one, before we discuss friends and friendship, we first need to talk about you.

Yes, **YOU**. Reading this book, sitting on your bed, wondering if there's anything decent for tea.

YOU. ARE. UNIQUE.
YOU-NIQUE.
U-NEEEEK.
YOU-NEE-KUH!

Got it?

There is no one the same as you in the entire world.

Imagine that.

Over seven and a half billion people. In fact 7,714,576,923 the last time someone counted (and that must have been a really boring job). And of all those billions of people, no one else is, has been, *or ever will be*, the same as you. For the whole of forever, to infinity and beyond, backwards and forwards and possibly sideways in time, you are the only, and most perfectly wonderful

YOU.

You are a fantastic human of the highest importance. You are as important as all the presidents and prime ministers and princesses of the world; as fantastic as any record-breaking Olympian, red-carpet film star or Insta-filtered influencer. You have as much right to be in this world as them and you matter just as much as any of them do.

You are also just as important as any one of your friends or family and anyone at your school, and that includes the headteacher and the kid who might get a trial for Wolverhampton Wanderers. That's right.

But the world is a funny old place. Sometimes it seems designed to make us feel like we are not as good as other people. In fact, sometimes it *is* designed to make us feel like we're not as good as other people.

Companies want to make money selling their stuff to us. If we all think we are fine as we are, *Thank You Very Much*, they will go out of business. They need to make us feel that there is something wrong and that we need to fix it.

If we could just be a bit ...

thinner CLEVERER FITTER

TALLER FASTER FUNNIER HAPPIER

OLDER PRETTIER SHORTER

BRIGHTER QUIETER

younger BRAVER LOUDER

BETTER

...then we would be fine, right?

WRONG.

Women and girls in particular seem to be targeted by this stuff, so we buy make-up to change how we look, perfumes and sprays to change how we smell, shoes to make us taller, and tons of stuff to make our hair curlier or straighter or shinier or redder or mermaid-ier.

All so that we fit in with some weird idea of what a girl *should* be.

Who gets to decide anyway? Who are all these people judging us by our appearance?

Well, if we're not careful it can be ourselves. If we start to believe that we are not good enough, that we need all this stuff to make us 'right', it can be like having our own personal mean girl in our head making snarky comments all day long.

'Your hair looks awful.' 'You're too fat.' 'You're too skinny.' 'You're too tall.' 'You're too short.' 'You're no good at sport.' 'You can't dance.' 'You'll never be any good at maths.' 'Your nose is too big.' 'Your lips are too thin.'

This is a horrible enough thing. But it almost inevitably leads to us negatively judging other girls too. As if by putting them down, we somehow move ourselves up.

None of this is any good for us or our friends, let alone our friendships.

To a certain extent it's natural to compare yourself with others, especially as you grow up. As we develop from little kids to adults, our brains go through huge changes.

The bit of our brain to do with self-consciousness, embarrassment and awareness of what others think of us becomes **HYPER**-sensitive. That's why we get so obsessed with what our friends think about us and why our mum's impression of Taylor Swift, which was so hilarious when we were five, is now a complete cringe-fest.

At the same time, a part of our brain, just behind our forehead, called the *prefrontal cortex*, can be a bit slow to wake up. This part of the brain is responsible for helping us take sensible, balanced decisions.

This makes for a rather unfortunate mixture that can lead us to take decisions so we can continue to fit in, even if we know they don't make sense in the long term.

For example, 'I know buying an expensive, frothy, sugary, iced drink from that coffee chain is going to use up the last of my money…which I need to buy my dad a birthday card…and I could get a drink at home for free. But

is getting one.'

But we can use logic and common sense to counteract this muddled decision-making. The first step is to stop judging ourselves. Yes, it's natural to want to be the best YOU you can be. But that's a personal thing.

For Ellie Simmonds, being the best she can be means power-swimming four lengths of an Olympic pool in under 3 minutes; for singer Rihanna, who has a phobia of fish and sea creatures, it might be paddling her tiny tootsies in five centimetres of water at the beach. Whatever is your personal best, aim for that; it doesn't matter what the person next to you is aiming for – they aren't in your shoes, or flippers or whatever.

Once you back off yourself and start to realise that you're pretty cool just the way you are, that's when the magic stuff happens – because, amazingly, other people start to think the same about you too!

You see, it's like a big circle. If you're a cheerful, optimistic person, who's not always blathering on about all the stuff that's wrong with her hair/skin/body/clothes etc, then you become much more fun to be around. And if you're more fun to be around, people want to be your friend no matter what sort of hair/skin/body/clothes you have.

Clever, eh? Learning to really like and be kind to yourself is like wearing a bright badge of love and fun that other people just can't resist!

Not convinced? Take a minute and think of the people that you know who are fun to be with. Do you enjoy their company because of their glossy hair and perfect test results, or because they make you feel good?

Remember, everyone else in the world is dealing with the same stuff. From the kid sitting next to you on the bus worrying that people don't think his trainers are cool enough, to the biggest Hollywood celebrity feeling awful about a bad review of her new film, everyone is trying to find their way through the judginess of the world.

So, let's cut each other some slack. Let's try to start making a difference. Instead of putting other girls down, let's all give each other a big pull up.

If the girls in your group start making negative comments about another girl, don't join in. Better still, say, 'I really don't think it's cool to say unkind stuff about people. Let's talk about something else.'

If you notice yourself thinking in a judgey way about the way someone looks or lives their life, gently remind your brain that, actually, this isn't going to help you be a good friend or a happy person. Accepting yourself for who you are and others for who and what they are is the best way of not getting sucked into the judgement trap.

And if we are less judgemental about others, perhaps they will be less judgemental about us. Win-win.

A very famous and talented writer called Maya Angelou suffered a lot from other people's judgement of her. She grew up in the USA at a time when it was legal to treat black people differently just because of their skin colour. She said,

'I've learned that people **WILL FORGET** what you said, people **WILL FORGET** what you did, but people will **NEVER FORGET** how you **MADE THEM FEEL**.'

Wouldn't it be amazing if we could all make each other feel good?

POPPYCAM

All this talk about judging and accepting people is making me feel really bad about what happened earlier today. I suppose I'd better tell you.

You see, I know what it's like to be new.

About a year ago, I joined a drama club. I'd wanted to go for ages since my cousin told me about it. It's at a small theatre on Saturday mornings and she said it was really fun and you learn loads about acting. I finally persuaded Mum to take me, even though it was a bit of a pain for her as it's in the next town. We arranged to meet my cousin outside, but just as we got there, my cousin texted that she was ill and wouldn't be coming after all.

I literally wanted to run away, but my mum said, 'I haven't come all this way to turn round and go home again, Poppy. And anyway, I've already paid.' She walked me in, said hi to the tutor, and then left me to it.

It was awful. I thought I was going to die of embarrassment. Everyone knew each other and everyone was staring at ME. I tried not to make eye contact with anyone by pretending I was finding my shoes really interesting to look at. I was terrified the tutor was going to make me pretend to be a tree or a duck or something.

But then we had to do a reading exercise in pairs. The girl I got put with was really funny and kept making me laugh. Then other people started talking to me and by the time my mum came to pick me up, I didn't want to leave. I was a bit unsure again the following week, in case everyone had had a personality transplant, but of course it was fine. Now I love it and go every Saturday morning, even though my cousin left months ago.

It's weird because at Drama Club everyone's different. There are different ages and races and backgrounds; there's a girl who uses a wheelchair and a boy with Asperger's but no one's treated any differently. Everyone seems to get along and accept each other, because we all love doing Drama. It's very different from school.

Anyway, I'm only telling you all this because of what happened today.

So, it's Wednesday morning and I'm just trying to find my homework in the bottom of my bag when Mrs Lambert claps her hands and says, 'Can I have your attention please, everyone? This is Mina.' She smiles at a girl with longish dark hair standing next to her. 'Mina's just joined the school, so I hope you'll make her feel welcome. We're very pleased to have you, Mina.'

'Thank you, Mrs Lambert,' Mina says. And she says it in a bit of a strange way. Like she has this really strong accent that isn't like anyone else's in school.

Izzy makes a bit of a snorty noise.

Mina stands at the front of class looking sooooooo uncomfortable. She does the finding-my-shoes-really-fascinating thing as well (although to be fair, she does have some quite cool shoes). While Mrs L witters on about what a wonderful school it is, Mina looks more and more self-conscious.

She eventually gets to sit down but the only spare seat is next to Mo Chaudhury, so unless she's seriously into Formula One racing, she probably doesn't get to chat much. A bit later, when the buzzer goes for breaktime, Izzy says, 'Glam Squad meeting over on the bench under the tree. We need to discuss my sleepover menu.'

I'm pretty sure that just means Who wants pepperoni and who wants margherita?, but of course I follow her over to the bench with everyone else. Izzy is fussing about lists and highlighters and who is in charge of popcorn and I look across the playground and notice Mina standing by herself. She's looking at the Fire Evacuation Procedure notice pinned to the school door as if it's the most interesting thing she's ever read.

'Shall we ask Mina to come over?' I say, 'She looks a bit lonely.'

Izzy looks up. 'Who?'

'Mina, the new girl. She hasn't got anyone to talk to.'

'Well that's because she's got a totally weird voice and no one can understand her,' Izzy says, and then she starts trying to mimic Mina's voice, and even though she sounds nothing like her, some of the girls start giggling.

'And have you seen her shoes?' Izzy says. 'So weird.'

'I think they're cool,' I say.
And then wish I hadn't.

Izzy looks at me as if I've just said I love broccoli sandwiches. 'They are gross, Poppy,' she says. 'They're all clumpy, they look like boys' shoes. And have you seen her schoolbag? It has a Hogwarts badge on it!'

'Yeah,' Bea says, 'I really can't deal with Potterheads.'

I make a mental note to take down the Welcome to Gryffindor Common Room sign on my bedroom door.

Jada says, 'And she's not coming to Izzy's sleepover so there's no point in talking to her.'

'Can we just get on with menu choices now, please?' Izzy says. 'My mum needs to go shopping tonight. Who likes garlic bread? Or shall we go for dough balls?'

But I can't stop looking at Mina standing on her own.

There are a few other groups of people hanging around, but no one is trying to involve her. She must feel so left out and awkward.

And then I make a decision. I take a deep breath, and I look Izzy right in the eye and I say, 'Look, I'm going to–'

'What?' Izzy snaps, like she knows what I'm thinking.

'I'm going to … have a margherita and garlic bread, please.'

I know, I know, alright?

But it's so hard being the one that stands up. Especially when everyone else is sitting down.

Angharad: Poppy shouldn't be so hard on herself. It is hard to stand up for what you think is right, especially when you're in a group situation.

Ruth: And at least Poppy thought about it. She had the right intentions, she just needed a little more courage.

Angharad: Yes. I think she'll feel better about things soon.

Bounce-Back-Ability

Ruth: Umm. Angharad. We've just received an email.

Dear **SQUF!**

I'm sorry but I have to hand in my resignation from the post of Guinea Pig.

I thought the idea was to help me fit in with the Glam Squad but now everything's gone wrong. I don't think your Super Psychology Secrets work!

I'm sending in my final video diary to show you what else happened today.

Yours squadlessly,

Poppy

Angharad: Oh dear. We'd better go to the PoppyCam.

All morning I can't stop thinking about how I would feel if I came to a new school and everyone ignored me.

Answer: Awful.

Then right before lunch we have one of Mrs Lambert's 'special' lessons. She's totally into nature, so once a month we get to go outside and write about or draw what we see (that means birds, leaves, insects and stuff, not the school wheelie bins).

As we are getting out our notebooks, Jada comes over to me. 'When we get outside, we're having an emergency Glam Squad meeting, over by the far tree,' she whispers. 'Mrs Lambert won't be able to see us there, and Izzy wants to decide which film we're going to watch on Friday, after we've watched Glam Girls.'

(I don't know why we bother. It will be Mamma Mia. It's always Mamma Mia because it's Izzy's favourite movie.)

As soon as Mrs Lambert lets us go, everyone rushes outside – everyone except Mina, who looks a bit uncertain about what she's supposed to do next. And I think about my brand, and about how horrible it is to be judgey, and I think maybe I'll just talk to her a little bit – quickly, without anyone seeing.

I should probably start off by apologising for not speaking to her earlier, but I'm not feeling that brave so I just say, 'Hi. I like your pencil case.' (Which is true – it's purple and has a built-in pencil sharpener – I'm a bit obsessed with pencil cases.)

And then a weird thing happens. Mina smiles, and I realise this is the first time I've seen her smiling. Smiling makes her look really nice and friendly. I get this nice warm feeling in my tummy too. She says, 'Thanks, my little brother got it for me for my birthday. Well, I think it was my mum really, but he gave it to me.'

And I think, her accent is fine. It's just a bit different. I don't know why Izzy was making such a fuss, it's easy to understand her. It's kind of cool, actually. We walk out to the school field and I say, 'I've got a little brother too. He's totally annoying.'

'Mine too,' Mina says. 'This morning he ate all the Chokko-Pops, again.'

And I say, 'Wait. Really? My little brother does exactly the same!'

Then we are both laughing, and I tell her about my excellent hiding place in the washing basket and we laugh even more.

It turns out Mina hasn't just moved schools, she's moved towns as well, right across the country. That's why she's got a different accent. She misses all her old friends and teachers. I tell her about when I went to Drama Club; I know it's not the same but I thought it might make her feel a bit better. Then I see this really cool butterfly.

'I think I'm going to draw that,' I say. 'I love butterflies.'

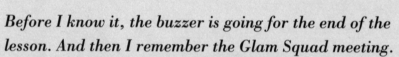

'I'm going to draw this leaf,' Mina says. 'I'd rather draw than write.'

'Me too!' I say.

Before I know it, the buzzer is going for the end of the lesson. And then I remember the Glam Squad meeting.

'I've got to go,' I say. But when I turn around Izzy is already by the door. She looks at me and does this sort of slow blink thing she does if you've said or done something she doesn't like, and I know I'm in trouble.

Back in class Jada sits down next to me and whispers, 'You missed the Glam Squad meeting,' making it sound as if I've just ignored an invitation to Buckingham Palace or something.

'I know,' I say. 'I kind of forgot.'

'We're going to watch Mamma Mia,' Jada says, 'After Glam Girls.'

At lunchtime I hurry out of class before Mina can talk to me. I don't want to be mean, but I can't risk Izzy seeing me chatting to her again, and anyway it's not as if she'd be allowed to sit on the Glam Squad lunch table, is it? But then before I can get to the lunch hall, Ms Harper, the headteacher, springs up from nowhere.

'Ah, Poppy. Just the person. Could you take these test papers down to Mrs Collins in the office for me, please?' she asks.

I take the papers but then at the office Mrs Collins is doing some important secretary-type stuff like an emergency paperclip order or something, and she makes me wait ages. By the time I get back to the lunch room, it's already full. I get a tray and there's only some dried-up fish fingers and the last soggy chips left, but they will have to do. Then I walk over to the Glam Squad table – and Amelia Munnings is in my seat.

Izzy looks up at me and says, 'Oh, Poppy,' as if she's surprised to see me. 'We didn't keep a space for you today.'

'But –' I look at Jada but she's pretending to be really interested in her chilli chicken wrap.

'Sorry, Poppy, but as you didn't come to the meeting, I've crossed you off the list,' Izzy says. 'And this table is only for the Sleepover Squad.' Then she gives me one of her

unsmiley smiles and says. 'You could always sit with your new Hogwarts friend.'

There's a horrible feeling in my chest, like I've been poked hard with a chopstick. And then I think I'm going to cry. So I just bite my lip and turn and head off in the opposite direction. Mina is sitting on her own and looks up at me as I pass.

'Hi,' she says. 'Do you want to sit with me?'

But I can't sit with Mina with everyone watching because they all think she's weird and then they'll think I'm weird too. I just push past her. There's nowhere else to sit and I don't care anyway because I feel sick. Behind me I hear Izzy laughing. I'm sure she's doing it extra loud so I can hear. I dump my tray in the clearing-up area and rush out of the hall.

And now I'm home. No one really talked to me for the rest of the afternoon, although Izzy did quite a bit of nudging and giggling and looking over at me. Even Mina didn't speak to me again. No one is answering my messages. I'm out of the Glam Squad, off the sleepover list and even Jada's not speaking to me any more.

So that's why I'm leaving **SQUF!**

Good luck finding a new Guinea Pig.

Oh Poppy! How horrible.

We understand you feel awful right now, but please don't quit.

This was something that probably had to happen sooner or later, but you stuck to your values and you should be proud of yourself.

We've got another **Super Psychology Secret** to talk about, and this might help. It's called resilience – or as we like to call it,

Bounce-Back-ability

Or, SHAKING IT OFF!

Remember that poor four-year-old at the beginning of the book? The one who was going to climb Everest, but then fell off the climbing frame and banged her knee?

Want to know what happened after she fell off? You didn't really believe she took up knitting, did you?

She had a bit of a snotty cry and her big sister dabbed her knee with an old tissue and said, 'Shall we go home?'

But this four-year-old took a deep breath, looked that climbing frame right square in the metal rivets and said,

NO!

This four-year-old marched over to that climbing frame and she put her foot on the bottom rung, and, even though she was scared, and even though her knee hurt like a big hurty thing having a really hurty day, she climbed up that measly piece of playground apparatus until she reached the top. And when she got there she planted a flag!

Well, all right, she didn't do that, but she felt like she had. She felt like she'd climbed a mountain. And, in a way, she had.

This four-year-old had bounce-back-ability!

Bounce-back-ability means being able to pick yourself up after a setback. It means staying positive, determined and on course when you get a problem or disappointment, or even a disaster. Bounce-back-ability means being able to look at a problem as a challenge to work through, rather than a reason to give up.

It is sometimes said that young people today don't have as much bounce-back-ability as young people did in the past, as if today's more comfortable lives have made them a bit soft and lazy, but then older people have always thought stuff like that. In 400 BCE (that's like, **SERIOUSLY AGES AGO**), the Greek philosopher Socrates is said to have written: 'The children now love luxury; they have bad manners, contempt for authority; they show disrespect for elders and love chatter in place of exercise.'

Which sounds exactly like something you'd hear on TV today. But just hold on a minute, Socrates.

Young people today have to manage a **HUGE** number of pressures that weren't around even twenty-five years ago, let alone two and half millennia ago.

Twenty-five years ago there was **NO SOCIAL MEDIA,**

NO SMARTPHONES,

NO INSTANT MESSAGING,

NO STREAMING,

NO BLOGGING,

NO HASHTAGS,

NO DIGITAL PHOTOGRAPHY,

there were only four TV channels, email was a crazy, exciting new idea, and the internet was just a tiny, weeny, baby internet-ling, babbling away quietly in the corner.

In the past, if someone had a bad moment, like forgetting their lines in the school play, it was only the audience in the room who saw it. Now it's quite possibly being live-streamed to the entire nation. So, don't tell us the young people of today have it easy, Socrates, you old windbag.

Developing bounce-back-ability is tougher, but also more important, today than it has ever been.

Having more bounce-back-ability is a good thing as it helps move us towards our goals, makes us feel more confident about our abilities and less likely to get overwhelmed by worry or sadness. It can help us with friendships too, as we learn to handle the ups and downs of dealing with those emotions in a more positive way.

No one is born being a perfect friend. It takes work to build a friendship and keep it going. Sometimes you'll have disagreements; sometimes you'll feel cross or hurt by something a friend has said or done; but if you're a resilient person, you won't let that floor you. And sometimes you too will do things that a good friend shouldn't do – you're not perfect either. No one is, not even Team **SQUF!** (Not every day. We're usually pretty perfect but there was a Friday morning. Once.)

Anyway, if you're upset because someone's been mean

to you, or because you've done something you wish you hadn't, you can either slink away and go live on a desert island with just a small parrot for company, or, if you've developed your resilient side, you can face up to the issue and sort it out, using your brain in thinking mode not just reaction mode.

SOME STRATEGIES FOR DEVELOPING BOUNCE-BACK-ABILITY.

1 BEEN THERE, DONE THAT.

Think about a time when you were upset by someone in the past. Think about what worked for you. Did you give it time? Did you talk it out? Did you just decide to put it behind you and move on? Either way, you got over it, right? Maybe it still hurts a little, but not as much, and you bounced back and got on with your life. See? You're a tough cookie. Ain't no one gonna keep you down. You've done it before and you can do it again.

2 LOOK AFTER YOURSELF.

If you've had an argument with a friend, give yourself

a break. You will have a lot of mixed emotions to deal with and probably won't feel like diving straight back in. It could be a break of a few minutes, like the climbing-frame kid, or longer if you're dealing with an emotional upset. Look after yourself by doing something you enjoy and taking your mind off the row. Self-care is very important. We need just as much, if not more, looking after when we are emotionally hurt as when we are physically hurt. But the good news is that emotional pain eventually passes, rather like physical pain – though it can be hard to remember that at the time. To make it all feel a bit more bearable, you need to be extra nice to yourself, acknowledging that you are having a tough time. Be nice to yourself in your thoughts. Talk to yourself in the way a lovely granny or a friendly, talking unicorn would. 'Take it easy, everything will work out', 'You're doing a great job at just getting through this day.'

Make yourself a hot chocolate, run a great, big bubbly bath, snuggle up on the sofa to watch your favourite movie, put on your favourite music very loudly and dance around the room. (Don't do all these things at the same time, or it is likely to get very messy.) If you're not sure what you need to do to look after yourself, think about the things you would say and do for someone you love and do those same things for yourself. Remember, it will all get better over time and by talking to others and spending time with radiators (people who warm you up) not sinks (people who drain you), you will slowly but surely feel better.

3 THINK – IS THIS GOING TO KEEP HAPPENING?

If your friend keeps being mean to you, maybe it's a sign that you need to find a new friend. If you've been shunned by the girl group, perhaps it's time to look at them as they really are. Do you want to hang out long term with a group of girls who treat other girls badly? Will you ever feel confident in their friendship? Although it's tough right now, you'd be better off finding some more supportive friends.

4 GET SOME PERSPECTIVE.

Ask yourself, 'Will missing out on the sleepover matter in a week's time?' 'Will it matter next month?' 'Next year?'

Usually discomfort, hurt or embarrassment is short-lived and things will feel better soon.

5 WORST-CASE SCENARIO.

Think 'What's the worst that can really happen here?' For example: you have an argument with your friend. Will you never be friends again? Will everyone in school stop speaking to you? Will you have no friends again, ever, and end up a strange old woman who lives in the woods and talks only to her canary?

Sometimes our brains create worrying pictures in our heads of all the things that could go wrong, when actually they're very unlikely to happen — and even if they do, you WILL be able to cope (that old lady actually *loves* where she lives!).

6 ACCEPTANCE.

You can't succeed at everything you try, and some things may just not be your cup of tea. Some friendships might not be your cup of tea either. Occasionally, you just pick up the wrong cup!

Sometimes you need to be strong enough to say, 'I'm not happy in this situation, and I don't want it to carry on,' and go to find something that suits you better.

When things get difficult, it is natural to want to curl up in a ball on a desert island and never have to face the world again. But there is only one way to get through tricky times – plough through them like a great big snow plough in mega-plough mode. Just like practising a sport is the only way to get good at it, you can't learn bounce-back-ability by thinking about it – you have to actually go through tough times to build up your bounce-back-ability muscles.

So, don't go all the way to that desert island. Curl up in your bed, put on your favourite music, have a good cry if you need to and then, when you feel that all the sadness and embarrassment has oozed out of you, go downstairs and make the biggest hot chocolate with squirty cream ever, so that your bounce-back-ability is all fuelled up. Your quiet time will help get you back up to strength.

And you *will* get back up to strength. Not as strong as you were before,

No matter how much of a tough time you're having, it IS get-throughable – and you're tough enough for the challenge. We promise.

POPPYCAM

REC

Poppy, you haven't really resigned, have you?

SQUF! needs you. Poppy? Poppy!

Hello. It's OK. I'm here.

Hey Poppy! You came back. You have bounce-back-ability!

Do I? I'm not so sure.

Last night I tried to think about bounce-back-ability.

I know that hanging out with Izzy isn't the best thing for me, because she always has to be in control of everything. But if I don't, I'll have no friends at all. How is that going to help?

The more I thought about it, the worse I felt. And then there's Mina. I wasn't very nice to her when she asked me to sit with her. I'm rubbish at sticking to my values. In the end I did what you said and made myself a hot chocolate with cream and mini-marshmallows. And then I cuddled Olaf and curled up in bed and fell asleep.

And this morning when I woke up, I felt fine ... for about two seconds, until I remembered everything.

I didn't even want to go to school. I tried the old tummy ache routine, but Mum only allows me one tummy ache a term. Then I thought I might go for the strange rash-on-my-arm-story, but my red felt tip has dried up.

Anyway, Mum was in a really bad mood because somehow a box of Chokko-Pops got mixed up with the washing and all the laundry got covered in brown sticky popped rice. It did smell nice though.

I tried to think about bounce-back-ability again, but I just felt miserable.

When I got to school it was no better. Jada has moved to sit near Izzy. She said, 'You are still my friend Poppy, but I can't really talk to you any more.'

Which is not really very helpful in a friend, is it?

So now it's break time. All the girls are over by the tree having a meeting. I didn't know where to go because

I didn't want to look at them all having fun, and I didn't want them seeing me on my own, so I slipped in here to the library.

And actually, it's kind of nice. It's peaceful and no one is bossing me around, or telling me I need a makeover. And I found a book that I've wanted to read for ages, so perhaps that's what I'll do, after I've sent you this video. I'll sit down on a bean bag and read. By myself. I don't feel quite so bad now. It's making me think that maybe I do have a tiny weeny bit of bounce-back-ability after all.

The book you have wanted to read for ages!

Well done Poppy. We're so glad you're back.

Bounce-back-ability isn't something that happens all at once, but if you keep on being a tough cookie, who follows the direction of her values, you will feel a bit better every day. Promise. And maybe our next

 ## Super Psychology Secret

can help too. We're going to talk about flexibility.

Ruth: Right. On your feet. Bend forwards and touch your knees. Now down to your toes.

Angharad: Err. Not that sort of flexibility. This is thinking flexibility.

Ruth: Oh good. My back hurts.

FLEXIBILITY
OR, THERE IS NO RIGHT OR WRONG WAY TO DO FRIENDSHIP.

Flexibility is as important for your mind as it is for your body.

If we expect things always to be just as we imagine they should be, we can become disappointed or even cross when things don't turn out as we hoped. Having a more flexible attitude to life can help us with our friendships by learning to see situations from different angles.

After all, people often do things that we don't expect.

Maybe your friend didn't reply when you messaged her last night, even though you really needed some information to finish your homework. Now you're going to be in trouble with your teacher.

If you think in a rigid way, full of all sorts of rules of how things should be done, you might get cross quite easily and quite often. You might think she has broken one of the friendship rules – after all, you always message her back straight away. You might even start to get all J.K. Rowling about it and weave a story around the situation; perhaps she did it on purpose so her homework would look better than yours; perhaps she wants you to get a bad grade; perhaps she secretly doesn't like you at all and is deliberately **PLOTTING YOUR DOWNFALL!**

But hold on a minute.

Maybe she didn't text you back last night because her mum told her to get off her phone; or she fell asleep; or something came up and your message went right out of her head; or she was just in a bad mood and didn't want to communicate with anyone. At all. Full stop.

Being flexible in our thinking means thinking of things from different angles and this can help us to feel less annoyed. It helps us to put ourselves in the other person's shoes and think about how they might be feeling, rather than just concentrating on how we're feeling.

So, if it's really bugging you, ask your friend why she didn't reply – but then accept her reason and move on. It's not a big make-or-break deal and your friendship is worth more than that.

The thing is, friendships are made up of humans (mostly... all right, perhaps your dog is your friend, but you probably don't message him about homework) and human friendships don't fit into a neat little box where everyone is consistently kind and thoughtful. No one is an excellent friend all the time, and perhaps there have been times when you have upset your friend unintentionally and never even realised.

So, **DON'T SWEAT THE SMALL STUFF**

as someone from California once said. In other words, don't waste all your energy fretting about minor problems.

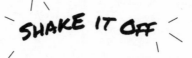

as someone from Pennsylvania once said. In fact, just as someone from Arendelle once said...

This doesn't mean you should accept people treating you badly. If things you don't like keep happening, perhaps it's time to let that friendship change and spend less time with that particular friend. Again, it doesn't necessarily mean one of you is wrong, or a mean person, but that you now have different things that matter to you in a friendship.

Take Jada and Poppy. Jada isn't deliberately being mean, but they want different things. Jada wants to chat about make-up and be in the Glam Squad. Poppy can either accept that and live with it, or decide this friendship is no longer working and move on.

What she can't do is control Jada.

And this is another way we can be flexible in our thinking. By realising that we can't control our friends, or life in general, and that things will change whether we want them to or not.

You may have heard people say

THEY DON'T LIKE CHANGE,

but you can bet they don't wear the same pair of socks for a month. (Unless it's your brother. Brothers live by completely different rules to the rest of the civilised world.)

What people really mean when they say *they don't like change* is that they get anxious about things they haven't experienced before.

This is another one of those natural things that our old cavegirl friends found useful. Being wary of new things helped keep them safe. If they found a plant they hadn't come across before, they needed to be careful in case it was dangerous to eat. The same with a strange animal or person. They had to be sure that new cavegirl coming down the path wasn't about to whip out a club and get all Neanderthally narky on them. (Right now, all over the country, history teachers are groaning in despair.)

In primitive cultures, **change** could be dangerous, and our good old brains made sure we paid a lot of attention to it.

However, once again this type of reaction doesn't help us so much today. While it's still not a good idea to eat random weeds (this includes school cabbage), it's a bit over the top to shout, 'Back away! She might have a dangerous concealed weapon!' when your teacher introduces a new classmate.

Not all change is bad. Imagine a world where nothing ever changed. The same dinner every day, the same music, the same TV programmes, the same clothes and the same people to talk to.

Life would be extremely

DULL.

So, while it's always going to be a bit scary to go to a new school or even get a new haircut, it's still the case that change makes life fun and exciting.

Being open to change and flexible in our thinking can help us in lots of other areas of our lives too. It can help us with school work and to get more creative ideas.

1 **THINK OF A SITUATION** where you've been annoyed with something a friend did. Now pretend for a minute you're the other person. Why do you think they might have acted like they did? Could there be other reasons that you haven't considered?

2 **IF YOU FIND YOURSELF GETTING PARTICULARLY HET UP** about the same thing over and over again, ask yourself what rule you have about it. For example, if your friend always arrives to meet you ten minutes late and it drives you crazy, ask yourself why.

Is it because you think she doesn't care about you enough to arrive on time? Is it because you've rushed your tea to get there and she can't be bothered to hurry?

Does your rigid brain say to you that it is

COMPLETELY
UNACCEPTABLE

for someone to act like this?

If so, you might want to thank your brain for trying to make sense of the world by creating all sorts of rules, but that actually the occasional ten minutes isn't worth worrying about and you're going to develop a whole new flexible rule: a rule that says instead of stressing about it, maybe you'll just leave a few minutes later, and listen to some music while you wait.

③ FOR FUN, TRY HAVING A 'DOING THINGS DIFFERENTLY' DAY. Make a list of things you could do. Clean your teeth holding the toothbrush in the other hand, have pasta for breakfast, wear odd socks, go to a different part of the playground at breaktime, watch a TV programme you never watch and eat a new food for dinner. This will help your brain to learn that change can be fun.

④ IF YOU HAVE A DECISION YOU NEED TO MAKE, TRY WRITING A LIST OF PROS AND CONS. On the left-hand side of the paper, list all the positive reasons for doing something and on the right-hand side, list all the reasons for not doing it.

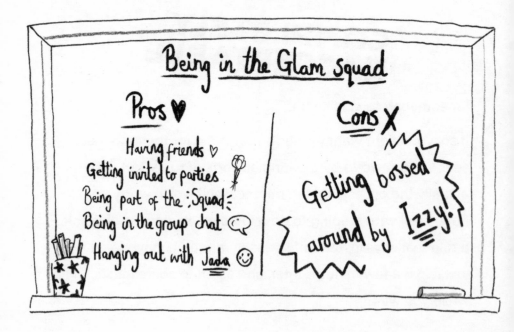

Now look at the list. What does it tell you? Remember, not all reasons are equally important, so it might not just be a case of counting up the 'votes' on each side. Perhaps you can see that there is no one version of what you should do, but different options to consider.

Staying **FLEXIBLE**

in our outlook means we can manage the ups and downs of life more easily. Like a sailor in a yacht, sometimes there will be flat seas and sometimes choppy ones, but if we learn to calmly keep our boat bobbing over the waves, we can get through any rough patches.

Oh good. Poppy's sent us Part Two of today's video.

POPPYCAM

REC

I sit on a bean bag in the corner and start reading my book, and before I know it the buzzer goes and I realise I've just had a pretty nice break time on my own, instead of standing under a tree being bossed around by Izzy. All through the rest of the morning Izzy is talking loudly about the sleepover instead of getting on with her work. Jada has brought a make-up palette in and keeps showing it off like it's a magical baby unicorn.

'Amelia I can't wait to give you your makeover,' Izzy says, glancing over at me. Perhaps she thinks this will make me annoyed, but it just makes me feel sorry for Amelia, who's definitely looking a bit worried too.

In fact, the more I think about it, the better I feel about the sleepover. I never really wanted to go, I just didn't want Jada to go without me. I miss Jada, but she's not the same any more. It does feel horrible being out of the Glam Squad, especially when they're all ignoring me, but at least now that I'm out of the Glam Squad, Izzy can't make me do things I don't want to do. Maybe Team **SQUF!** is on to something. Everything changes and some of it is not nice, but not all changes are bad.

But then it's lunchtime. I have to go into the lunch room all on my own, like a total Milly-no-mates. I get a tray and stand in the queue. Izzy has just got served and she looks at me and then comes over.

'Poppy,' she says. 'I've decided you can come back in the Glam Squad. Like, as a trial.'

'Really?' I'm so surprised I almost drop my tray.

'You can't be like a senior member though, you know, deciding what we do and stuff. You have to do what we say. And you have to come to all the Squad meetings. And stop talking to weird girls.'

'Right.'

'I haven't decided if you're still invited to the sleepover yet. I'm going to think about it. But you can come on the lunch table today if you want.' And she picks up her tray and walks off.

I look over to the Glam Squad table. Jada is looking at me and nearly smiling, but then she turns back to Izzy.

The queue shuffles forwards and I don't know what to think. I should be pleased, I suppose. I'm one of the girls again. That's a good thing, right? I don't have to be on my own at break times and I might even get to go to the sleepover. And then the queue shuffles forwards a bit more and I think about that list of Pros and Cons. There were a lot of Pros to staying in the Squad. And only one thing on the 'Cons' side. As the cook dollops some chewy-looking pasta onto my plate, I make a decision.

I take a deep breath, pick up my tray and walk over to the Glam Squad table.

'Thanks for letting me back in the Squad, Izzy,' I say.

'It's only a trial, Poppy.'

'But I'm kind of OK as I am.' I can hardly believe I've just said that. For a moment I feel like I'm dangling precariously from a high wire.

Izzy doesn't speak. She just frowns and then her mouth sort of hangs open with no words coming out and I see a bit of pasta stuck to her teeth. And then, even though my cheeks are burning and  *I feel a bit sick, I turn around and walk away.*

There might have only been one thing on the Cons side but that one thing was getting bossed around by Izzy and, even though it's only one thing, I know it's the most important thing. I've got to stick to my values and be my real self.

I see Mina sitting on her own again and I walk straight over to her.

'I'm sorry about how I was yesterday,' I say. 'Can I sit with you?'

Mina looks up, surprised. 'Yeah. Of course.' And she grins. 'As long as you don't mind me being weird.'

'I don't think you're weird at all,' I say, sliding into the seat. 'Well, maybe just a bit.'

And then she laughs and I laugh, and it's kind of nice not to have to worry about laughing at the wrong time or saying the wrong thing. We just eat our food and chat about stuff. Mina tells me all about the small town she comes from, and guess what? It turns out that she's really into stars and stuff. The space kind, not the Glam Girls kind.

'Where I lived before was a small place, the sky was really dark at night and you could see millions of stars,' she says. 'I miss that. One day I'd like to get a telescope.'

'I love looking at the stars,' I say, and then I tell her about the grains of sand on the beach thing.

'Wow. That's totally awesome!' she says.

'I saw a shooting star once,' I say. 'It was amazing.'

'I've seen them too,' Mina says. 'Did you make a wish?'

'Yes. But I was only seven so I wished for a pet unicorn.'

'Did you get one?' Mina laughs.

'Not yet,' I say.

Then we both start giggling. Suddenly, there's a screechy sound as Izzy pushes her chair back really noisily and heads for the door, and all the Glam Squad follow her.

She walks past my chair and says, 'You need to grow up, Poppy!'

I'm a bit shocked. But then I look at Mina and we both burst out laughing again.

None of the Squad spoke to me this afternoon, not even Jada. But instead of getting upset or angry, tonight I tried to think myself into Jada's shoes. I think she just wants to be accepted by the Squad more than anything else. I suppose that's just up to her. I can't control her, just like Izzy can't control me. Everyone has to do their own thing. And mine and Jada's things are not the same any more.

And I even felt a bit sorry for Izzy. I know she's had a tough time over her mum and dad splitting up. She just wants to be in charge and the other girls don't mind. But I don't fit in with her way of doing things.

So tonight I'm at home but I'm not sitting, crying and cuddling Olaf. I'm drawing a picture of a shooting star flying through the stars and planets to give to Mina tomorrow.

That's great Poppy. By trying to be more flexible in your thinking, you've made some really tough decisions. You stayed on-brand by putting your values into practice, being true to what you believe (**HONESTY**) and by thinking positively about your relationship with Mina, Jada and Chloe (**FRIENDSHIP**). You also practised being assertive and used your logical thinking (rather than emotional thinking) to figure out what would be better for you in the long term. Putting up with some short-term discomfort when you stood up to Izzy meant that you felt better yourself this evening. You've used all of that brain power to understand that Jada is not a bad or a good person, she is just someone trying to figure out herself too. What great Super Psychology Secretising! Enjoy your evening.

Ruth: Well it seems that, at last, everything is going right for Poppy.

Angharad: I know. We haven't heard her say

for ages.

Bully Tactics

POPPYCAM

REC

Oh no! What's happened, Poppy?

Those girls!

Today is Friday, sleepover day. All the girls have brought their sleepover stuff in and they're all being really loud and giggly about it. Well, everyone except Amelia. She just looks a bit lost, like she's not sure she's allowed to join in. Izzy makes everyone hand over the sweets they've

brought so she can be in charge of sharing them out. She put them all in this big carrier bag and keeps waving them about like she wants everyone (mostly me) to see.

'We're going to have such an excellent midnight feast,' she says.

I probably should ignore her but she keeps going on and so I say, I don't care how many sweets you've got, Izzy.'

But it is totally bad timing as Mrs Lambert is just walking past.

'I'll take those, Isobelle. No sweets in school,' she says

and takes the carrier bag out of Izzy's hand.

Izzy says, 'What? You can't take our sweets, Miss!'

'You can have them back at the end of the day,' Mrs Lambert says. 'If I remember. Now sit down, please.'

Izzy hisses at me, 'Mrs Lambert had better give us those sweets back, Poppy, or I'm holding you responsible,' and stomps back to her table. All morning she keeps giving me evil looks.

At break, Mina and I hang out together but the Glam Squad keep staring at us across the field. Even Jada. In the end we make an excuse that we need to use the toilet and go back inside until the buzzer goes.

At lunchtime, I give Mina the shooting star picture.

'I thought you could make a wish on it. For your telescope, not for a unicorn.'

'I love it, Poppy,' she says. 'You're so good at drawing, you should do it more often.'

'Yes. I think I will, now,' I say.

The Glam Squad are all being loud about the sleepover again, and Izzy is doing even more lists. They all get up and walk out past our table, ignoring us. Well, pretending to ignore us, except Izzy happens to say,

'My mum's bought cookie dough ice cream,' really loudly just as they pass and all the girls go, 'Wow!' and 'Yum!' And 'I can't wait for tonight, it's going to be sooooo much fun.'

'I'm not allowed dairy,' says Amelia.

'Oh Amelia, you're so lame,' Izzy says, and Amelia looks worried again.

When we get back to class Mrs Lambert is talking about the class trip. 'I'm open to ideas,' she says. 'Any suggestions for this year's trip?'

'Pleasureworld Theme Park,' someone shouts.

'Goldwater Shopping Mall,' comes another shout.

'I think we need something a little more educational,' Mrs Lambert says with a frown.

'Could we go to the Science Museum?' I say. 'They have loads of space stuff.'

Mrs Lambert looks pleased. 'That's an excellent idea, Poppy. I'll speak to Ms Harper about it later.'

There's lots of excited chatter, and I grin at Mina. But then Izzy leans over to me.

'What did you say that for?' she hisses. 'Who wants to go to a museum?'

Then Bea says, 'My little brother likes space stuff – he's five.'

'Well, Poppy's still basically a little kid,' Izzy says. 'She's still got her cuddly Olaf at the end of her bed, haven't you Poppy?' And they all start laughing.

'How do you—?' And then I realise. Jada. And I get that horrible feeling in my chest.

Jada sort of opens her mouth and then closes it again and looks out of the window. I can't believe it. The old Jada would never have given away secrets.

'Settle down, please,' Mrs Lambert says with a frown.

Mina pulls me by the arm. 'Come on, Poppy. Let's sit down.'

At home time, Mina and I hang back a little as the girls are all shrieking and gathering up their stuff. Mrs Lambert gives Izzy her sweets back, then they all pile out to Izzy's mum's car which is waiting outside.

We pick up our stuff and Mina rummages in her Hogwarts bag. 'I just want to make sure I've got my picture,' she says.

Then she gasps and holds it out to show me. Someone has written Grow Up Losers! right across the middle of it.

'Nooo!' I say. 'That took me ages. It's ruined!'

Mina sighs, 'That's so childish,' she says.

I take the picture from her and throw it in the bin.

Oh! Those girls!

Mean and bullying behaviour is the **WORST!**

When people pick on us, it can often feel as if there's nothing we can do to about it. True, we can't control someone else's behaviour. But there **ARE** things that can help.

1 THE FIRST THING TO DO IS TO GET CROSS. It is **NOT ACCEPTABLE** for someone to hurt you or treat you in a mean way. No one has the right to do that and you must decide you are not going to stand for it. Channel your inner cavegirl and get into sabre-tooth scaring mode. Wave your imaginary club and roar,

'NO WAY AM I TAKING THIS!'

into the bathroom mirror.

If you are putting up with bullying behaviour from anyone, then resolve right now that you are going to get it sorted.

2 BULLYING TAKES DIFFERENT FORMS.
If someone is physically hurting you (hitting, hair-pulling etc.) or constantly upsetting you with harsh comments, then it may be obvious that you need help to stop it. But sometimes people pretend they're being funny when actually they're

being unkind. They can say things like, 'It was only a joke,' or 'It's just banter!' which make it sound as if it's your fault for being upset. Trust how you feel. If you feel a knot in your stomach or you want to cry or you want the

ground to swallow you up, when someone 'jokes' with you, then that *is* bullying, however much people say it's just a little laugh.

3 TALK ABOUT WHAT'S GOING ON

– to parents, teachers and friends. Yes, it's hard. Bullies rely on making you feel that you have no support or way out, and may even warn you not to speak up. **But if no one knows, they can't help.**

Bullying is always against school rules and in many cases against the law.

All schools have to take it very seriously. Parents and teachers may surprise you by being more helpful and sensitive than you think. Even if the person you've told can't do anything directly, just having someone to listen can help you feel better and come up with a plan. Look at the next chapter on communication for ideas to help you speak up.

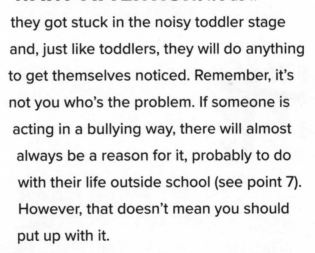

4 PEOPLE OFTEN BULLY BECAUSE THEY WANT ATTENTION. It's as if they got stuck in the noisy toddler stage and, just like toddlers, they will do anything to get themselves noticed. Remember, it's not you who's the problem. If someone is acting in a bullying way, there will almost always be a reason for it, probably to do with their life outside school (see point 7). However, that doesn't mean you should put up with it.

The advice people give for both tantrumy toddlers and boisterous bullies is often the same, *ignore them*. This is a very easy thing to say, but a very hard thing to do.

After all, if they've got you in a headlock you're going to notice. Also, *ignore them* doesn't mean you shouldn't tell anyone (see above).

However, if the bullying is verbal (using words), then there is a bit of sense in ignoring it. If you can find a way to limit the attention you pay to someone who's picking on you, they will often get bored and seek their 'attention fix' elsewhere.

Unfortunately, they will probably get louder before they finally head off – just like a little kid screaming and throwing all their toys around before they finally fall asleep in the corner. So, find some ways to help you keep your cool and direct your attention elsewhere. Search for something

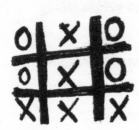

in your bag, read a book, look at your phone, do the 16 times table in your head – whatever it takes to distract you while they're going on and on. In the end, they will scuttle away.

5 PEOPLE CAN DETECT FROM A PERSON'S POSTURE AND BODY LANGUAGE HOW THEY'RE FEELING and how they think about themselves. If you think about it, this is true. It's pretty easy to tell if your friend is unhappy or down – if she is slouching along like there's an invisible wet towel draped over her head, you can be pretty sure she isn't on top form. When she's in a positive mood she stands up straighter, looks people in the eye and has a spring in her step. As it's easier to pick on someone who's feeling vulnerable, making it obvious from your body posture that you're feeling worried or low is a sure-fire way to attract unwanted attention. A simple but effective way of managing bullying is to adopt a confident posture. Stand up straight, shoulders back and keep your head up. Without doing anything else, this gives off the signal *'Don't mess with me!'* Often a small show of strength is enough to make those cowardly creeps back off.

6 PEOPLE OFTEN PICK ON THE VERY THING THAT WE ARE MOST UNSURE OR UNHAPPY ABOUT.

Izzy knows Poppy will be embarrassed about Olaf, and that she will be hurt that Jada has given away her secret, so she uses these things to get at her.

And the moment you start worrying that your new glasses don't suit you, you can be sure that some Snidey Sally will say 'Why did you choose those? You look like my Grandma.' The thing to remember is that the bully is saying this to you because they

know it's your weak spot, **NOT BECAUSE IT'S TRUE**. If you let them continually get under your skin, they are getting the reaction they want.

But how do you stop them getting to you? Some people find it helps to imagine they are wearing a superhero suit which no mean word-arrows can pierce. Or that they have their own invisible forcefield which protects them from nasty comments. As the forcefield comes down, have an appropriate theme tune in your head, the theme from *The Avengers* maybe. Now you are invincible! Let their words ping off your armour so they don't get inside your head and become part of how you think about yourself.

7 HAPPY, CONFIDENT PEOPLE DON'T BULLY. They have no need to. At heart, bullies are insecure and unsure of themselves and will try to make up for this by bringing other people down. Often they have unhappy home lives, where they are pushed around themselves. This doesn't mean we should excuse the bully's behaviour, but maybe it helps us understand it a little better.

Again, the problem is with them, not you. Even though it's hard to really hold on to this idea at times, it can help you to realise that bullies are not all-powerful superhumans. They are, in fact, the opposite.

8 **ALTHOUGH IT MIGHT BE TEMPTING TO HIDE AWAY** in your bedroom, try to spend as much time as possible with people who really love and like you (even if that means your annoying brother). This will remind you what a fantastic person you really are, and stop the bully chipping away at your confidence.

9 **YOU MAY HAVE BEEN IN A SITUATION WHERE SOMEONE ELSE WAS GETTING BULLIED AND YOU STOOD BACK AND WATCHED WITHOUT HELPING.** This is called being a 'bystander', and this

behaviour can be as hurtful as the bullying itself.

Or maybe some of your friends are 'bystanders', too scared to stick up for you when you are being picked on. Talk to them about how it makes you feel when that happens. They may never have looked at it that way and will be shocked to know that they are making things worse. Work together to figure out how to stand up for one another.

10 WHAT IF YOU HAVE BEEN INVOLVED IN BULLYING SOMEONE?

Does this mean you are a bad person? No, but it means you have done something that's unkind and wrong. You need to think about why, and how to put it right. Luckily, it's never too late to change our behaviour. Spend a bit of time working out why you behaved that way. Did it make you feel big or cool? Did it make you feel part of a certain gang or group? Are you jealous of the person in some way, and putting them down makes you feel better? When you've thought about why you got involved, you should be able to recognise if these feelings start cropping up again. Talk to someone about it, and about how you can handle your feelings. Remember, hurting someone else physically and emotionally is

NOT ACCEPTABLE

no matter how much we want to fit in.

Can We Talk?

Let's get back to Poppy to find out what happened when she got home.

POPPYCAM

REC

I get home and I have just about had enough of today. But as I get in the door, my mobile pings. There's a message from Izzy. Part of me doesn't want to open it, because I know it's just going to be her showing off about how great the sleepover is, but I can't seem to help myself.

It's a video of the Glam Squad – all except Amelia, I guess they're making her hold the camera.

'Hi Poppy,' they shout and then they all start singing 'Do you want to build a snowman?' before collapsing into heaps of laughter.

I bite my bottom lip. I'm not going to let them make me cry. I shut down my phone so I don't have to see any more messages.

I need to cheer myself up so I think I'll have a hot chocolate and then do Mina another picture; drawing always makes me feel better. But when I get in the kitchen there is no hot chocolate left. Just an empty jar in the cupboard.

'Did you have all the hot chocolate?' I snap at my little brother, who has a tell-tale brown moustache.

'Yep,' he says with a grin. 'I had two cups.'

'Then you're just a selfish, annoying, little pain!' I yell.

He looks at me a bit shocked, then his chin wobbles like he's about to cry.

'Poppy!' my mum says, coming into the kitchen.

'That's not very nice. I hope you don't talk to your friends like that.'

And something inside me just goes BOOM. Before I know it, I'm stamping up the stairs shouting. 'You don't know anything about me! I don't even have any friends! You never even listen anyway!'

And I bang my door shut and throw myself down on my bed. Then I get up again and take Olaf and throw him out of the door. And then I slam my door again, throw myself on the bed and have a massive cry.

After about ten minutes, there's a knock at the door. I look up and expect it to be Mum, but when the door opens a crack, it's Olaf's head that pops round. 'Can I come in?' he says, in a very Mum-like voice.

'That's not even funny,' I say.

Olaf comes in with Mum right behind (all right, with Mum carrying him). Mum sits down on my bed. 'Olaf was worried about you,' she says.

'He's just a stupid, childish toy,' I say.

'Oh. Cover your ears Olaf!' Mum says, putting her hands on each side of his head.

'I don't think snowmen have ears,' I say.

Which makes Mum laugh, and me, a bit. 'Is this about the sleepover?' Mum says. 'Or the non-sleepover. I notice you still seem to be here.'

'Izzy crossed me off the guest list,' I say.

'What about Jada?' Mum says. I don't know what to say so I just shrug. Mum's kind of good at getting body language, though.

'It seems like you and Jada have been drifting apart for a while now,' she says. Then she sort of frowns. 'Is there something else you want to tell me?'

I want to tell her about the video and about them writing on the shooting star picture and about not being able to sit on the Glam Squad table, but I don't even know where to start. And if I show her the video, what if she phones Izzy's mum up? Or goes to see Ms Harper on Monday? That'll make everything even worse. I don't know what to do.

> *'I tell you what,'* Mum says. *'Why don't I make us both a drink and we can get to the bottom of things.'*
>
> *'Alright,'* I say.
>
> *'Tea OK? I don't think there's any hot chocolate left,'* she says, winking at me.

Oh dear.

Poppy is having a really rubbish day! But luckily, she has her mum onside. Now she needs some help to say what's on her mind.

Families often get the brunt of things when we are in a bad mood. Psychologists call this 'projection' – when we want to make other people around us feel bad like we do. The thing is, Poppy is not really that cross with her brother or mum. Maybe they've both been a bit annoying, but not in a way that deserves all that shouting and banging about. Unfortunately, we often use the people closest to us as a way of letting off steam. No matter how much she shouts and bangs, Poppy knows deep down that her mum and brother aren't going to kick her out of the Family Squad.

But even though she's upset and angry about stuff at

school, it's not really fair of her to be unkind. In fact, in a funny kind of way she's acting a bit like Izzy!

Perhaps Izzy's parents splitting up has made her feel uncertain and out of control of the events happening at home. Her way of making herself feel better is by being super-bossy at school. The reason she picks on Poppy so much might be because Poppy won't go along with the others and Izzy feels challenged by this.

Whatever the reason, getting in a massive row usually ends up with us, and everyone around us, feeling even worse.

The secret to getting your family to help and support you before it gets to explosive stage is

– finding ways to talk things over that work for everyone.

That's why parents are often so keen on getting everyone to have a family dinner. It might seem a bit annoying if you have to stop whatever you're doing right in the middle, just to come and have your tea with your family, when you could easily have it later, but those times sitting around the table are a good time for everyone to catch up. You can talk about school or what's happening in the holidays. Does anyone need a lift this week? Has Dad remembered to book you in for a haircut? Can we work out a fair way to share the Chokko-Pops? Does anyone know a good way to get chocolate out of laundry? All sorts of things. And because everyone's stopped doing other things for half an hour, they tend to take more notice.

But having a meal together is often not practical. People have sports, clubs and other appointments. Parents might work shifts or get home late. So, finding other ways to communicate is important. Lots of families have group chats and message boards, which are great for day-to-day stuff, but for more important things we need to talk face-to-face.

Parents are usually excellent people to speak to about friendship problems. Mums were once girls themselves and have a lot of experience around making and managing friendships. However, not everyone has a mum, and not every mum is helpful. Grans, big sisters, aunties and teachers can all be great listeners too. And even dads have their good days – they can be great listeners, if you get them in a quiet moment.

Talking with friends usually comes more naturally, but there are also times you may need to say something awkward there too. If your friend smells a bit whiffy after a PE lesson, it's probably better to say, 'Would you like to borrow my body spray?' rather than go in with, 'Urrgh. Get away from me. You smell like a drain blocked with mouldy cauliflower cheese!' And then there are those really difficult conversations when you're upset with someone but don't know how to tell them, or you need to apologise but can't find the right words.

So, whether you're trying to tell your friend that you're upset because she never invites you round to her house, or you just need to tell your teacher that you don't understand the maths homework, having a few handy hints can help.

SQUF! Handy Hints for Having a Happier Heart-to-Heart

1 THE FIRST THING TO REMEMBER IS THAT COMMUNICATION IS A TWO-WAY PROCESS. It's not just about you, sorry. You're going to have to do some listening. Sometimes when someone's saying something, especially something you don't like, it's tempting to jump in and disagree – but if you hear them out, you might find there's some sense in what they're saying.

Even if you disagree, you can't persuade someone to your point of view if you don't know what they're thinking.

And if you don't let them finish what they're saying, they're likely to become frustrated and not listen to you either.

2 **CHOOSE THE RIGHT TIME.** It's no use trying to explain a long, complicated problem to your mum as she's on the way out of the door to her Hot Zumba class. If you don't know when's a good time, ask. Try saying something like, 'Is there a good time for us to talk about something later, Mum?' (Or Nan, Miss, etc.)

3 **IF THERE'S SOMETHING COMPLICATED YOU NEED TO SAY, AND YOU'RE WORRIED YOU'LL FORGET, TRY MAKING A FEW NOTES.** Writing things down can often make us feel better anyway; it gets stuff out of our heads and puts us in control of our thoughts.

4 **TALK FACE-TO-FACE.** Texts and messages can be easy to misunderstand because humans need to see body language and facial expressions and hear tone of voice to help us understand each other properly.

 That's why emojis were invented, to try to replace facial expressions because everyone was getting so confused!

No matter how many emojis you use, if you have something important to talk about, it's always better to do it in person.

5 **TALK SIDE-BY-SIDE.** Car journeys are great for chatting things through. Sometimes it feels easier if you don't have to look right at the person you're speaking to. Plus, it means your mum can't run off to put a load of washing on just as you're getting to the important bit. Walking the dog is another good time to discuss something, and picking up the dog poo makes for a nice natural break in the conversation.

6 **IF YOU'RE WORRIED** that your mum will go haring off to school to talk to your teacher or be on the phone yelling at someone else's mum before you've managed to get your point across, tell her. Before you start, ask her to promise she won't do anything without you agreeing. That way, you can come up with a plan together.

7 **NO ONE CAN READ YOUR MIND** (well, maybe Dynamo can, but unless he's your dad, keep reading). Sometimes we think people understand how we're feeling when really they

Mind Reading Helmet

haven't got a clue. That's why sulking is pointless, because the other person may not know what you're sulking about, or may not even notice! So, tell them how you're feeling. And if you don't understand how they're feeling, ask.

8 **YELLING IS LIKE THE OPPOSITE OF SULKING.** It's one of those cavegirl-type reactions, useful for scaring off marauding mammoths, but not an effective way to communicate. It just means everyone else starts yelling to make themselves heard and before long you've got a full-on Yell-a-thon and no one's getting their point across.

If you find yourself getting angry, take five. Say, 'I just need a break for few minutes because I feel like I'm getting cross.'

9 **IF YOU START A SENTENCE WITH 'YOU,' SUCH AS SAYING, 'YOU NEVER LISTEN!'** or 'You're so selfish!' it's sounds like you're blaming the other person and they're likely to leap in to defend themselves. However, there is a smarter way to say the same thing that makes it ten times more likely they'll listen. Instead of starting with *You*, try starting with *I*.

'I feel sad when you're too busy to listen.' Or, 'I really wanted some hot chocolate and I'm upset because you took it all.'

10 **IF SOMETHING'S BOTHERING YOU, TALK ABOUT IT EARLY ON, SO IT DOESN'T BECOME A BIG DEAL.** 'I don't mind you borrowing my highlighter pens, but I'd prefer it if you ask,' is always better than, 'What are you, some sort of serial stationery stealer!? I'm padlocking my pencil case!'

11 **DON'T BE AFRAID TO APOLOGISE IF YOU'VE DONE SOMETHING HURTFUL OR WRONG.** EVERYONE has upset someone at some time or another. However, 'I didn't mean to', 'It wasn't my fault', 'Soz', 'Ooopsie' and the really annoying 'I'm sorry if you got upset about ...' are NOT apologies.

If you need to say sorry, say

It takes a little bit of courage, but it helps everyone to move on.

Plan - Tastic!

POPPYCAM

SQUF!

Hi Team **SQUF!** Here's the second part of tonight's video. Your Handy Hints came in really useful.

Mum bustles around the kitchen carrying two cups of tea with a bar of chocolate in her teeth and a packet of biscuits balanced on her elbow, which is quite impressive. If she ever needs a new job, they'd probably take her on at the circus.

'Mum,' I say, 'first of all, I need to say something.'

REC

Mum looks at me expectantly, while trying to lower the biscuits. I take a deep breath.

'I'm sorry if you were upset ... No, what I mean is ... I shouldn't have shouted and slammed stuff. I didn't mean to ... So soz ... Well. Actually. Sorry.'

Phew. That was quite hard. But Mum smiles, and drops the chocolate.

'Thanks Pops. That's very mature of you. And I'm sorry for snapping at you too.'

She puts down the drinks and gives me a hug. Everything seems much better already.

'Now was there something you wanted to talk about?'

'Yes. But will you promise not to do anything that I don't agree to?'

Mum frowns. 'Yes, I suppose.'

So then I tell her. All about Izzy and Jada and the Glam Squad. And about not being allowed to sit on the table or go to the sleepover, and about Mina and the picture ... and then I show her the video.

'Oh Poppy. That's awful.' She jumps up. 'Do you want me to speak to Jada's mum? I'll come up to school. And if I see that Izzy, I'll have something to say too!'

'Mum! You promised!'

'Oh yes. Right.' She sits down again. 'Well. Well…
we should make a plan.'

'What do you mean, a plan?'

'When I'm at work, if we
have a particularly difficult
challenge to solve, we have a
team meeting and come up with
a plan.'

'Right.'

'We work out a) What do we need to do? And b) How are
we going to do it?'

'But this isn't about work, Mum. This is just Glam
Squad stuff.'

'Same process,' Mum says. 'We just need to work
through it.'

This sounds good. Mum stands up and hands me my
pencil case. 'You take notes,' she says and starts pacing
up and down. I've never really seen my mum like this.
She's very … professional. Maybe there is something to
this planning.

'Okay. First thing. What do we need to do?' Mum says.

'Stop Izzy picking on me.'

'Good,' Mum says. 'And how are we going to do that?'

'I don't know,' I say. 'That's the point.'

'Well, if your brother was doing something you didn't want him to, what would you do?'

'I'd just tell him not to.'

'So, perhaps you could tell Izzy.'

'What?!' I thought my mum might have a good idea but obviously she just doesn't get it. 'That's a stupid idea. She'd never listen.'

'Try. Next time she's mean to you, tell her to stop. Tell her you'll report her if she does it any more.'

'I can't do that!'

'Why not? What have you got to lose?'

'That would just make her worse.'

'Would it? Come on. Give it a try. You can practise on me. Stand up tall and look me in the eye.'

Partly to stop her going on, I get up from my chair. I look at her but I can't say the words. 'I just can't, Mum. I'm not that brave.'

'Pretend you're doing it in Drama Group,' Mum says. 'Pretend you're, I don't know … Merida from Brave … or Hermione Granger … or Taylor Swift! What would she say?'

And actually that seems to work – if I think about someone strong and brave doing it, I feel like I can do it too.

'I've had enough of you picking on me, Izzy,' I say. 'If you do it any more, I'm reporting you.' I can't believe I'm doing it, but it feels kind of good.

Mum claps her hands and laughs. 'You see?! Now write it on the plan.'

I write.

'Now, what else do we need to do?' Mum says, pacing around like Sherlock Holmes on a mission.

'Umm. Stop them sending me messages?'

'Well, that one's easy,' Mum says, and hands me my phone.

I open the group chat. There are six more messages. I look at Mum and she nods at me. I leave the chat and delete the messages.

Mum attempts to give me a high five, but it's a bit awkward when I've got tea in one hand and a phone in the other. 'If they try to bother you again you can block them,' she says. 'Put that on the plan too.'

'But now I'm Squadless!' I say.

'True. But there's no point being in a mean Squad. How about inviting Mina round tomorrow?'

'Really?'

'Yes. We can have a take-out. Your choice. Put it on the plan.'

'This is all easy when you're here, Mum. I'm not sure I can manage it at school, though.'

'What you need is some support. You've got Mina to help but you really do need a teacher to know.'

'I can't! What if they get told off? Then they'll be even more mean.'

'If you'll let me, I can have a private word with Mrs Lambert.'

'No way!'

'I can explain that you have a plan to get things sorted out in your own way, but at least she'll understand the situation. Then, if there are any more problems, she can support you.'

'I don't know.'

'Don't worry. I'll make sure it's not a problem. We both want you to be happy at school.'

'Well, OK. As long as no one sees you talking to her.'

Mum finishes her tea while I tidy up the plan. It was very simple really. I'm not sure it will be that simple to carry out, but I do feel loads better.

Mum picks up the cups.

'Well, I'm glad that's all sorted. Oh – there is one more thing you need to do.'

'What's that?'

'Apologise to your brother.'

POPPY'S PLAN

1. Tell Izzy that I've had enough and I'm going to report her. Eeeek!
2. Block the Glam Squad if they keep messaging me.
3. Invite Mina to come round.
4. Mum to speak privately to Mrs Lambert.

HOW TO MAKE A PLAN

We can sum up making a plan very simply.

First, *what do we need to do?*

And secondly, *how are we going to do it?*

But there are a few steps to getting it right.

1 BE CLEAR WHAT THE PROBLEM IS.

Is it that your friends are not including you when they talk about the latest TV series, or is it that, because you don't like the programme, you don't want them to talk about it all the time? Think about the problem in a rounded way.

Is someone, perhaps including you, being inflexible or judgey?

② WHAT OPTIONS ARE OPEN TO YOU?

Accept that there are things you can't change and things you can. Look for the simplest solution first – this is often the best. But be prepared to think creatively to give yourself other options.

③ GET HELP. If possible, get another person

to help you think it through. They may have ideas you haven't thought of and they will support you as you carry out your plan.

④ WRITE IT DOWN.

Using a journal or somewhere you can write privately, set down the steps you are going to take. Writing things down helps to get them out of your head and you can clearly see what you need to do next.

⑤ BE BRAVE. Take the first step

towards solving the problem. This could involve being assertive, it could be about accepting that one friendship has finished and you need to move your energy towards a new friendship, or it could be about apologising.

6 GIVE YOURSELF SOME BIG RESPECT.

You have done a very hard thing. You've taken control of a situation and are working towards solving your problem. You didn't let the situation floor you and you have proved your bounce-back-ability! Well done!

All Together Now

POPPYCAM

REC

Hi, Team **SQUF!** *My week is up. I hope I've been a good Guinea Pig.*

You have done so well, Poppy! We can't believe it was only a week ago when we first met you. And perhaps things won't be quite as

from now on.

It's a bit scary thinking about talking to Izzy on Monday, but now I've got Mina and my mum to back me up, I feel a lot better.

Will you come back in a few weeks to tell us how things are going?

Sure. See you then.

Angharad: I'm going to miss Poppy.

Ruth: Me too. She was a true great amongst guinea pigs.

Angharad: Do you think she'll be OK on Monday?

Ruth: I think so. She's found out a lot about friends and friendships.

Angharad: Let's have a super **SQUF!** recap.

We've learned that friendships can change, often quite quickly and this can leave you shocked, upset and feeling out of control. None of these are nice feelings, so we try to combat them by behaving in certain ways – by being overly nice and allowing our values to get trampled over; by being moody and unkind; or just by wanting to curl up in a ball. But the best way to deal with the tricky patches of friendships is to try to stay calm and communicate clearly.

Let's look at all the things Poppy did to make changes, and how they could help us too.

1 ON-BRAND. Poppy thought hard about what made her, her. She decided her values were *creativity*, *friendship* and *honesty*. And that meant she wasn't a compatible friend with someone who didn't really value those things.

Find out your brand. What makes you, you? What makes you proud to be who you are? Hold on to these values because they will anchor you when the going gets tough. Knowing your brand means you can be more sure of what you want to do and what you don't want to do. In the end, people will respect you more for this.

2 STAND-UPPY. Poppy had to find the courage to stand up for her new-found values. She also realised that being yourself and standing up for yourself are not easy options, but it's better than feeling bad about what you've done.

Learning to be assertive means you're not shy about letting other people know what you want or don't want. This isn't being bossy, it's being comfortable stating your feelings.

3 ACCEPTANCE. Poppy had to accept that she hadn't always acted as kindly as she could, especially when Mina first arrived. But she put that right because she accepted that everyone is different, and that's a good thing.

Differences are not a threat, they're an opportunity. If we are open to these differences in ourselves and in others, life is much more interesting.

4 BOUNCE-BACK-ABILITY.

Poppy found rejection by the Glam Squad really tough, but she worked on her bounce-back-ability. She learned that we gain more bounce-back-ability by keeping on going through the tough times. The more resilient we become, the more it will benefit us in the long run.

Bounce-back-ability means that, yes, you feel upset and worried, but you don't let yourself be overwhelmed by these feelings. Using all the superhuman strength you have, you keep going, pushing through the bad times to get to the better times ahead (and there are **ALWAYS** better times ahead).

5 FLEXIBILITY.

Poppy had to find out that, even if you are a good friend to someone, changes happen and we can't always control them. She had to let go of her old friendship and realise that changes can be positive as well as negative. It's all part of the friendship journey. Being flexible means that you understand and accept that things change, people change, teachers change, the weather changes. It's good to have some rules for life, but when we expect everything to stay the same, we can get upset and disappointed.

Stay super-bendy flexible, so that you don't get too hung up on one idea of how things should be. Welcome changes into your life, and lots of positive things will happen.

6 COMMUNICATION. Poppy overcame
her awkwardness and found a way to talk to her mum about what was happening.

We need to be brave and ask for help sometimes. Learning to communicate effectively with your family and friends is a great way to make sure your feelings are understood and to get the right support when you need it.

7 MANAGING THE BULLIES.

Ooh. This was a tough one. Sometimes it's best to ignore bullies, especially on the internet where you can (and must!) block them and delete them. But Poppy also had to deal with Izzy being mean to her in school.

Having the courage to stand up to someone mean is not easy, but it's the only way to let them see you're not going to let them push you around. Stand tall and speak up.

8 MAKING A PLAN.

Poppy made a plan to help her get control of the situation. Writing things down often helps us to get things in perspective, to see patterns and ways forward. She used simple problem-solving skills of thinking 'What do I need to do?' and 'How can I do it?' And she got the support of another person to help her find solutions.

Good Luck

Girls are amazing! When we find a group of friends (or even just one friend) who truly gets us and lets us be our real self, it can be the gateway to great times. Good friends will have fun with you, laugh with you, support you when you're down and cheer you on when you succeed.

Managing those relationships takes a bit of work at times. Although **SQUF!** can't be there with a PoppyCam for everyone, we hope the ideas in this book will help you through the rough patches. Remember, everyone goes through friendship problems, and the bad times will always pass. Don't hang on to relationships that are bringing you down; sort them out or move on.

You're super-special and you deserve a super-special squad.

GO FIND YOURS!

Epilogue
One Month Later

POPPYCAM

REC

Hey Team **SQUF!** *It's me, Poppy.*

Poppy! How are things going? It's been a whole month since we heard from you.

I know. I've been pretty busy. I'm sending through my final video.

So, a lot has happened this month.

Mina comes around all the time now. We have pizza and play music in my room. Sometimes we go to her house and watch Harry Potter films. We completely do not do makeovers. I've drawn her another picture of the shooting star and she has it above the desk in her room. In fact, I do a lot of drawing these days.

The Monday after the sleepover, Izzy came over to me at break with a big smirk on her face and said, 'We had a great time on Friday, Poppy. Did you get our video?'

'I deleted it,' I said.

'Aww! Did you not like our singing?' Izzy said.

My mouth was really dry and my hands were sweaty but I knew I had to be brave and follow my plan, so I stood up straight and said, 'Don't talk to me any more Izzy. If you pick on me again, I'll report you to Ms Harper.'

Then Mina stood up and said, 'We both will.'

Izzy's mouth twitched and then she just said, 'Losers!' and walked off.

I was really shaky when I sat back down, but I felt better. Like I wasn't just letting her get away with it.

And it worked! She actually did keep out of our way. Although she gave me mean looks all the time, she stopped coming over and saying stuff. She didn't even comment when Mrs Lambert announced the trip to the Science Museum.

Then something else happened.

One day at lunchtime, I saw Amelia Munnings standing on her own after she'd collected her lunch and looking uncertainly over to the Glam Squad table. Then she took a couple of steps towards it, but even I could see there was no seat for her. Priti Begum was in her space. I could see Amelia biting her lip and not knowing what to do. Izzy said something to her and she looked like she might cry.

I knew exactly how she felt. I looked at Mina.

'Should we?'

'I think so,' Mina said.

'Amelia,' I called. 'Do you want to sit with us?'

Of course, once Amelia started to hang out with us, Izzy tried to start picking on her too. But this time there were three of us to tell her to back off. And actually, now there are four. Priti Begum sits with us as well. She only lasted a couple of days in the Glam Squad before she got fed up with all the arguments.

So, you see **SQUF!** did work. I found my Squad!

It wasn't the Squad I thought I wanted, it's a new one — but it's much better.

We're the Odd Squad, and that's just how we like it!

Thanks for your help. Keep on **SQUF!** -ing!

Ruth: Our work here is done.

Angharad: Goodbye Poppy.

Team **SQUF!** OVER AND OUT.

Index

PILL 03-09-2020

Paperback: 978 1 5263 6241 4
Ebook: 978 1 5263 6242 1

THIS BOOK WILL (HELP) COOL THE CLIMATE

50 WAYS TO CUT POLLUTION, SPEAK UP AND PROTECT OUR PLANET!

BY ISABEL THOMAS
ILLUSTRATED BY ALEX PATERSON

Discover how YOU can cut stinky fumes, and tread more lightly on the planet. Become an eco-warrior, not an eco-worrier, with 50 practical tips to really make a difference!